less then

10

This book is to be returned on or before the date above.
It may be borrowed for a further period if not in demand.

Essex County Council
Libraries

love songs

love songs

CRASS

POMONA

A POMONA BOOK P-004
Mad in England!

Published by Pomona 2004

1 3 5 7 9 8 6 4 2

Pomona Books
PO Box 50, Hebden Bridge, West Yorkshire HX7 8WA, England, UK
www.pomonauk.com

Distributed in the UK by Turnaround Publisher Services Ltd,
Unit 3, Olympia Trading Estate, Coburg Road, London N22 6TZ

A CIP catalogue record for this book
is available from the British Library

ISBN 1-904590-03-9

Set in 10 on 13.5pt Granjon
Typeset by Christian Brett

Printed and bound by Biddles, King's Lynn

Let me say, at the risk of seeming ridiculous,
that the true revolutionary is guided
by great feelings of love.

— CHE GUEVERA

CONTENTS

FOREWORD   XI

PREFACE   XIX

ACTS OF LOVE   I

REALITY ASYLUM   51

WHERE NEXT COLUMBUS?   54

BIG A LITTLE A   57

A MESSAGE TO THATCHER...   60

YES, SIR, I WILL   63

HOW DOES IT FEEL?   92

THE IMMORTAL DEATH   95

DON'T TELL ME YOU CARE   98

SHEEP FARMING IN THE FALKLANDS   102

GOTCHA!   106

WHO DUNNIT?   108

NAGASAKI IS YESTERDAY'S DOG-END   111

HAVE A NICE DAY   113

NINETEEN EIGHTY BORE   115

WHAT THE FUCK?   117

WOMEN   119

BEG YOUR PARDON   120

REALITY WHITEWASH   123

BIRTH CONTROL & ROCK 'N' ROLL   125

PUNK IS DEAD   127

NAGASAKI NIGHTMARE   129

DARLING   131

MOTHER EARTH   132

MOTHER LOVE   134

POISON IN A PRETTY PILL   136

OUR WEDDING   138

BERKERTEX BRIBE   139

SMASH THE MAC   141

BATA MOTEL   145

DON'T GET CAUGHT   148

SYSTEMATIC DEATH   151

THEY'VE GOT A BOMB   154

SENTIMENT   158

MAJOR GENERAL DESPAIR   160

FIGHT WAR, NOT WARS   163

DEMONCRATS   164

CONTAMINATIONAL POWER   166

SO WHAT?   168

SYSTEM   171

BIG MAN, BIG M.A.N.   172

HEALTH SURFACE   174

YOU'VE GOT BIG HANDS   176

TIRED   178

RIVAL TRIBAL REBEL REVEL   180

CRUTCH OF SOCIETY   182

THE GASMAN COMETH   183

DEADHEAD   185

HEARD TOO MUCH ABOUT   187

THE GREATEST WORKING CLASS RIP OFF   188

HURRY UP GARRY   191

WHITE PUNKS ON HOPE   193

TIME OUT   195

FUN GOING ON   197

SUCKS   199

ANGELS   200

REJECT OF SOCIETY   201

END RESULT   203

CHAIRMAN OF THE BORED   205

I KNOW THERE IS LOVE   207

WALLS   209

UPRIGHT CITIZEN   211

BUY NOW PAY AS YOU GO   213

SMOTHER LOVE   215

YOU CAN BE WHO?   217

BUMHOOLER   220

YOU'RE ALREADY DEAD   222

BLOODY REVOLUTIONS   225

GENERAL BACARDI   228

DRY WEATHER   229

SHAVED WOMEN   231

G'S SONG   232

YOU PAY   233

SECURICOR   235

WHAT A SHAME   237

RIVAL TRIBAL REBEL REVEL (PT. 2)   239

WHO'S SIDE YOU ON?   241

MEDIA BAG   242

I AIN'T THICK, IT'S JUST A TRICK   243

BANNED FROM THE ROXY   246

DO THEY OWE US A LIVING?   248

ASYLUM   250

THE SOUND OF FREE SPEECH   253

10 NOTES ON A SUMMER'S DAY   255

FOREWORD

A BEAUTIFUL SUNNY DAY. T-SHIRT WEATHER ALREADY AND it's only March. Fallen branches snap under foot. The light filters through the trees and is hazy around us. A man passes by walking his dog.

"Good morning."

It's an understatement.

Christian (Pomona designer) and me are heading for Epping town centre. It's somewhere over there—past the fields, trees, hedges, motorway bridge and, finally, schools and housing estates. We've just spent a night with Penny and Gee at the *Crass house*. We come to a pond in a clearing. It's teeming with life, water lilies and pond mint, crane flies and cabbage whites. We both feel unusually happy. It's not just the sunshine and the summer-to-come. We're talking about Crass, the influence they've had on our lives, reminiscing about when we first discovered them, gigs we went to, people we knew. It's taken 20 years, but visiting the house, meeting them, feels like a circle closed. We'd traced the source of a large part of ourselves.

. . .

When I was about 15, someone in my class at school drew a cartoon of me in their rough book. The speech bubble coming from my lips read: 'Crass, Crass, Crass, Crass, Crass.' I was a sensitive kid and the piss-take hurt. I hated that anyone saw me as this tedious, one-dimensional character saying the same thing over and over again, over and over again. I'm not so hard on myself now. In fact, I like that I was obsessional, up to my eyeballs in it. And Crass had that effect, there were no half-measures.

I'd lived a typical working class provincial life until Crass. There had been few books around the house. The pictures on the wall were plastic-framed prints of seascapes and sad clowns. Mum (not dad, *as if*) fed us on fish fingers and Arctic Rolls, never pasta, spaghetti or beans you didn't buy in a tin. I had all the love in the world but I didn't have discussions about art, politics, literature, poetry or philosophy. A few of us — the quieter ones, I suppose (and it's the quiet ones you need to watch out for) — had gravitated to one another at school. All from the same background, wondering just how big and wide a life could be. Someone somehow discovered Crass and, at last, we'd found our epiphany and our totem: the rest, our former lives especially, was history.

Crass were the utmost. Loudest, fastest, hardest, most fundamental. The music was an unrelenting stop-start cacophony. If you listened hard enough though, the structure was actually quite conventional — intro, verse, chorus, verse — and it soon made sense. The effect was the same with the lyric. They were screaming bloody murder at meat-eaters, fascists, liberals, Jesus Christ, do-gooders, bigots, capitalists, the media, communists and The Clash (who had exposed an inherent hypocrisy of their revolutionary stance by signing to a major label). They blow-torched the lot, headstrong and sloganeering but in the scrabble of lyric, information and artwork, they were also cerebral and poetic.

They performed under pseudonyms in sublimation of their egos; pressed their own records and sold them cheaply; refused to speak to the music press; carried their own musical equipment and amplifiers; drank tea instead of beer; had people of all ages in the band; pre-advertised a specific date when they would split up to avoid any undignified lingering; appeared at village halls and scout huts. Every rock 'n' roll stereotype was eschewed, which, paradoxically, made them the most valid, thrilling definition of rock 'n' roll ever. They wore black clothes and were like a salvation army moving through Britain, picking up kids, lifting off the top of their heads, stirring up their brains and leaving them walking their hometowns shell-shocked. Crass were irresistible because they were an authentic revolution, challenging and confronting all that had gone before.

They spawned hundreds of satellite groups, many of whom were showcased on their *Bullshit Detector* compilation albums. I bought a guitar and within two weeks had formed a band, Untermensch, and released an 'album' on cassette. Our manifesto was formed by Crass and one of their apostles, Andy T, who turned out (bizarrely) to live less than half a mile away from us. His track, *Jazz on a Summer's Day*, had a huge impact, both in its sentiment and the do-it-yourself ethos it summarised. While he speeded up and slowed down a jazz record, Andy spoke deadpan into a cassette recorder (in, *would you believe*, a Lancashire accent):

'Life is what you make it
Music is anything you want
You don't have to be able to play
You don't have to have something to say
Just do it.
Fucking do it.'

I still play it every two or three years. Andy's voice is full of defiance and self-belief and when I hear it again it reminds me to be strong and also of those times, us all being friends and realising it was okay to write poetry and stories and not have to hide our intelligence and sensitivity, as we had during most of our childhood.

Crass were avowed anarchists and while this was open to various interpretations, to me it transmuted to self-belief and compassion for others, an absolute respect for freedom:

'Be exactly who you want to be, do you what you want to do.
I am he and she is she but you're the only you.'
    – *Big A, Little A*

Untermensch became a fanzine as well as a band. We devoted the centre-spread of our first issue to Crass. There were other groups of course, but Crass' position as cultural and political superiors was unequivocal. The Sex Pistols, The Jam, The Clash, Buzzcocks etc all had energy and some great songs but fell considerably short of Crass' authenticity.

Our heartfelt articles were typed on to strange double-sheeted paper that was horrible to the touch, dry and smelling of charcoal. The school had a *community officer* who organised tea dances for pensioners and helped the mums and toddlers group with their leaflets. He had a beard and wore sandals with socks underneath. He agreed that we could use the school duplicator to print the fanzine but noticed the swear words.

"Look lads, I don't want to impinge on what you're doing or anything, and it's great that you're doing something positive with your time, but could you spread your *fucks* out a bit? If they're all in one place, we might get a few complaints."

. . .

It used to be fanzines, now it's books, which is probably a decent metaphor of life. *Love Songs* is an attempt to restore Crass to the agenda, to remind people who may have forgotten and introduce them to people too young to have been around at the time. They stand a revisit and a re-evaluation because they were important. They changed lives and might do so again.

Reading through the lyrics once more, I'm struck by how acutely they summarise a critical historical period. I'd forgotten (thankfully) the sheer bleakness of the early 1980s. If Crass appear to be reduced to hysteria and neurosis in places, it is with good reason. Death really did feel to be everywhere. We were led to believe that nuclear war was imminent. The countdown had begun and we were seconds from midnight. There were marches and badges, films and documentaries: mushroom clouds, bodies snagged in barbed wire fences, Hiroshima, Nagasaki—coming to your town soon. A car door slamming on the next street might be the aftershock of a fallen missile. We'd soon be stock-piling rings drawn from the fingers of the dead and comforting shaking, wide-eyed women on the streets like in the film, *The War Game*. The conflict hadn't even started but you felt you were suffering from radiation sickness.

Three million people were unemployed. Factories were shutting down and you never heard of anyone getting office jobs back then. This was relentless and had the effect of suffusing you with hopelessness, like placing a polythene bag over your life. Meanwhile, at school, if you aspired to anything half-decent, they took it as arrogance or that you were kidding yourself, living on dreams. There didn't seem to be anything worth growing up for: rainy days, sleeping in, spaghetti hoops for dinner, television, a walk around the shopping precinct in the afternoon, home for tea, more television, back to bed, waiting for the bomb to drop.

At least you now had Crass on your side, reporting back from all this misery but also nurturing hope and individualism, a way out. Their anger is palpable in the songs, an anger borne from suffering the consequences of other people's greed and selfishness. All these years on, I am still angry too, that fear of the bomb and fear of the future blighted my childhood and early adulthood. Margaret Thatcher rises from her sepulchral majesty in these lyrics too and I am reminded of my hatred of her: the dogma; condescension; the sense that she was the embodiment of evil—unfeeling, uncaring, contaminated. She used the Falklands War of 1982 to forge herself as the Iron Lady, understanding that a lust for blood would foster patriotism and ultimately secure her more power. Crass saw through the sham of the 'war' and, quite rightly, it became the subject of several songs included here.

. . .

The sequence of lyrics in *Love Songs* does not follow a time chronology. We decided upon an order that we felt was more suitable to a book format, looking to create different moods, rhythms and vary the subject matter.

It is probably best read over a few sessions. It is intense and relentless and assails the reader. I like this effect, thoughts provoked from bombardment. The energy still crackles. Much of it is frighteningly prescient — foretelling of the grip of conglomerates, the idolatry of wealth etc. Of course, with a menu so rich, it is important to disseminate, think for yourself beyond the holler. Back then, I remember some 'fans' becoming dogmatic about Crass, revelling in the austerity and viewing every line as an irrefutable truth. I thought the idea was to question, think for yourself, and if that meant disagreeing with a Crass viewpoint, so be it. They covered a lot of issues. A total accord would surely have been evidence of a pliant mind. I was (and still am), for example, troubled by their stance on religion. In most places their anger is righteous but here they seem spiteful. They gorge on Christ's status as a symbol of guilt, which is part of their function as iconoclasts, but they choose to over-look the happiness and succour he brings to millions. And all those great buildings and pieces of art!

The feminist text of the album *Penis Envy* probably had the most lasting impression. It has informed my thinking on women and womanhood. I imagined it being a starting pistol to scores of albums and bands developing the theme but sadly it sits pretty much in isolation in my record collection. It had felt like we were getting to somewhere good, but sexism is now a thriving adjunct of consumerism and it seems fair game to exploit, ridicule and objectify both women and men. I resent that I have to explain to my kids why a naked woman is leaning over the bonnet of a car ("She looks like a dog!" one of them cried recently) on a giant billboard poster. Clearly, we've gone backwards here.

. . .

Back to the Crass house. The walls and floors are crooked. It feels like you're all at sea. Gee is warm and chatty. Later she'll drive us into town and tell us about a performance artist whose partner cuts him on stage with a razor blade. She thinks it's 'strangely beautiful,' the blood patterns across his skin, his bravery and honesty. She's very matter-of-fact. She could be telling us that the local bakery has a new line in scones. In the house, she shows us a book she's working on, where she's stuck animal heads on to people in old black and white photographs. Christian thinks it's brilliant. Profound even. I'm not very good with art. I imagine showing the book to my dad and his response. I want to laugh. I wanted to laugh at the performance artist too. Gee said it took a few days for him to heal. I imagine him on a 30-date tour, all of them consecutive and with afternoon matinees in local schools. What a bloody mess! I'm not very good with art.

Penny is variously tending his garden, prodding at the open fire and, well, brooding. He seems tormented. He's halfway through a book, a poem, a life. Perhaps he's spent too much time discussing art, politics, literature, poetry and philosophy. Maybe I should go careful with the assumptions. Keep an open mind, or else! His hair is tatty and he's wearing those trousers that stop just past the knees, almost-shorts. *The Face* should ask him to model the next time it decides peasant chic is in vogue. He has this very serious, quite intimidating face but when he smiles it's just about the best smile you'll ever see, eyes dancing, happy lines all over the place. While he's jamming logs into the fire I notice that the skin on his legs is that of a much younger man: all this insurrection must be good for the flesh. He has extraordinary charisma. Strength of character and self-belief glows around him like a barbwire halo. We chat on relatively deep levels but I sense that, as I talk, he is three thoughts and six ideas removed, on to somewhere else.

Later, I'm struck by how fantastic it is that these people, so palpably different than us, have had such an influence on our lives.

So much was galvanised from this wonky house where the members of Crass each spent some time. I've read somewhere that they sold more than a million records, imagine that.

While I'm there, I don't think of this legacy and I'm not over-awed (as I thought I might be). I keep thinking how trusting they are, and kind, letting us into their home, feeding us, and that although they're opinionated and sometimes prickly, they're also — and there's only one word for this really — loveable, which was the whole point.

Mark Hodkinson
Pomona

PREFACE

IF TWENTY-SIX YEARS SOUNDS LIKE A LONG TIME, OVER A quarter of a century sounds more like an eternity, but either way, that's how long ago it is since Steve Ignorant and myself started messing around with ideas which very quickly developed into a band. In those days Steve, who was young and working-class, was mildly bored, while I, who was older and middle-class, was very angry. Apart from our ages, nothing much has changed, but in the interim we created Crass and since then have suffered the consequences. It seems to me that anything involving more than two people and which sustains itself for more than two days stands in grave danger of becoming an institution, and Crass was no exception. When eventually we had expanded to become a full band, we gave ourselves a sell-by date; we'd shut down in 1984, which, Big Brother or no, gave us seven years to change the world, and the rest of our lives to de-institutionalise ourselves. I'm still trying, although just recently I've gone full circle and got back into world changing. I'll bet you've noticed the difference.

When in 1977 I first heard Johnny Rotten's call to arms, I was aware that something was going on, but instinctively felt that it was just another case of rock 'n' roll tokenism. *Anarchy in the UK*? I didn't really think so. Rotten after all had already written his own epitaph, *'get pissed, destroy'*, which is precisely what The Pistols did to themselves; one big hedonistic orgy in which Sid's death was the biggest buzz of all. As McLaren admitted in a last-ditch stand to capitalise on his fast-dying assets, it was just another rock 'n' roll swindle. Yes, Malcolm, and just about as radical as a good old British Rail sandwich: plenty of plastic wrap and no content.

There can be no argument that punk was a kick-back against the velvet and patchouli complacency of the dope-hazed Sixties and early Seventies, while for the music business its ugly face meant no more than a much needed boom: regardless of quality, to maintain profits, fashions have to change.

Riding comfortably on the back of the Tories' *'never had it so good'* catchphrase, the hippy dream had in most respects been dependent upon the economic stability enjoyed in the UK of its day. Once recession cut in, the dream went sour. Ironically, rather than being a reaction against the 'hard times' of mass unemployment, poor housing and failing social services which now existed, and rather than contributing to the atmosphere of growing political unrest, punk as conceived by McLaren and his merry men merely followed traditionally establishment interests of élitism and personal gain, interests that the various members of The Pistols were either too young or too stupid to reject.

From panto stage to tabloid page, The Pistols promoted an aggressive form of individualism which, rather than advancing empowerment and dignity, simply gave licence to self-indulgence and all its inherent dangers; twenty-five years on, McLaren's sneer and Sid's death seem pathetically synonymous (if not even symbiotic).

So, from the outset it was clear that The Pistols were no more than puppets manipulated by cynical string-pullers McLaren and Westwood, whose tacky emporium, 'Sex', clearly demonstrated their motives: *'just another cheap product for the consumers' head'*.

The Pistols' lamentable Crystal Palace gig of 2002, mounted to coincide with the anniversary of the Queen's Jubilee, was the final nail in the coffin, if a final nail was still needed: *'schoolboy sedition backed by big-time promoters.'* Nice try, boys, but no. The Pistols' unwarranted fame can easily be explained in that it reflected the nihilistic self-interests of the media that had so lauded them. The servant best serves the master who best serves the servant, but this time around no one was really taken in. However, a couple of days before the gig, alongside the predictable tits, bums and cultural illiteracy, Rotten addressed the nation through the pursed orifice of Murdoch's fetid arsehole, *The Sun*:

"I said this thirty years ago, the only true anarchists in Britain are the football hooligans. They're the only ones that actually do something."

Maybe from the luxury of his Los Angeles home, our Johnny hadn't heard of the anti-globalisation protests, the Peace Not War Collective, the Animal Liberation Front, Reclaim the Streets, the Greenham Women or indeed of any of the manifestations of genuine anarchic thought and action spawned by Crass and like-minded bands and people, but that's to jump the gun.

So, in 1977, Steve was bored and I was angry; he could just about sing and I could just about play the drums, and that seemed a good enough reason to start a band. At that time I was working on a long poetic rant entitled *Christ's Reality Asylum*, but it didn't seem to fit too well to a back-beat and, in any case, Steve thought it pretentious. So, off he went and wrote *So What?*, which fitted a backbeat, but which I considered a bit simplistic. For all this, Steve and myself very quickly learnt to accommodate each other's foibles — it was easy, he stuck to singing and songwriting, while I stuck to drumming and thinking my own thoughts. We agreed that with his background he was better equipped to write the kind of songs we wanted to play, which suited me just fine; I could get on with my poetry.

Bit by bit we were becoming a band; Andy (BA Nana) turned up having nicked a guitar (which, to his credit, he never learnt to play) and nudged his way in, while those of possibly greater talent hovered on the edges wondering how best they might contribute to the general cacophony. Some fell by the wayside, but most anyone who wanted to be a part of the action was welcomed with open arms. As interest grew in what we were up to, so we realised that we had given birth to a hungry monster which, although as yet nameless, was vociferous in its appetite for new material. The monster needed songs to survive, and so, taking a leaf out of what I thought might be John Betjeman's approach to rhyme and rhythm, I started writing; it took the addition to the band of Eve Libertine for me to be able also to pursue my more avant-garde leanings, the first offering being *Reality Asylum*, a rewritten and shortened version of my poem *Christ's Reality Asylum*. Steve was not happy.

One year later, having named the monster 'Crass', we released *Reality Asylum* as our first single (an Irish pressing plant having refused to include it on our first album). Within days of its release we received a visit from Scotland Yard. We'd been tipped off that the Vice Squad were on their way, but had quite reasonably imagined that it was some kind of punk outfit coming round to check us out.

"We believe that one of you is responsible for the record that I hold in my hand. Is that so?"

Silence.

"I should warn you that anything you say will be taken down and could be ... "

Our lips were sealed, and from that time on, throughout the various court appearances that peppered our musical career, where we couldn't remain silent, we diligently refused to break the code of anonymity that now surrounded our work. Everyone and everything was either Crass or nothing at all, right down to our underpants, all of which were black and all of which at one time for some inexplicable reason disappeared beneath Pete Wright's bed. Pete was our bassist, but that didn't seem to me to be a good enough excuse. It was winter, we were in the middle of a one week's tour and I was pantless and pissed off. Steve had the good common-sense to nick a pair from our sound engineer's suitcase; they were very baggy, pale blue Y fronts. I wouldn't have been seen dead in them, and I told Steve as much. "That's 'cos you ain't got no taste, mate," was his riposte.

It was the unusual mixture of age, class, gender and taste that set Crass apart from the rest. Most bands were (and are) culturally one-dimensional. Crass wasn't. For example, it was the women in the band who ensured that what hitherto had been a primarily ladish outfit took on board the issue of sexism. It was they who insisted that we dropped a favoured rhyming couplet, arguing that whatever the National Front might be, they were most certainly not a part of female anatomy. We recanted, but, nonetheless, runt never did seem to have quite the same ring to it (no pun intended). On the matter of couplets, I've never bothered to add up how many times we used pit with shit or, indeed, shit with pit, but I'm certain that it was far too often. It became rather a joke between us, one about which we felt a certain degree of embarrassment, and one which the music press picked up on with what was probably justified critical zeal. "Gumbie activism," was one attack that I rather enjoyed. Eat your heart out, Mr Betjeman.

From the start, the music press actively disliked Crass, which, of course, compounded our dislike of them, but as we weren't playing their game, why should they play ours? "Crass", they decreed, "are too serious." Which, in a way, we were. However, it seems ironic that twenty-five years and two Gulf Wars down (watch out for the next instalment) that our seriousness should now increasingly be seen to have value. I've lost count of how many radio, television and press interviews I have done over the last few years, but it seems that our political views, once reviled by the media, are now respected enough to command air-space. Gee's artwork (unscrupulously imitated and ripped-off, but rarely acknowledged) has become the subject of academic debate, and there's even a growing interest in the never before recognised musical intelligence of our work. We weren't fools then and we're not fools now, but it's taken an awful long time for the mainstream to wake up to the fact.

Crass were a diverse group of artists, writers, film-makers, musicians, activists and drop-outs sharing a communal lifestyle deep in the Essex countryside. Whereas Rotten's call for 'Anarchy in the UK' had been little more than a hollow nihilist groan (and where's my percentage?), to us it represented a battlecry. For over a decade the various members of what became known as Crass had been involved in exactly the free-thinking anti-commercial ideology the McLaren clique were now attempting to exploit as a commodity. We believed that you could no more be a socialist and signed to CBS (The Clash) than you could be an anarchist signed to EMI (The Pistols) and we set out to prove the point. Having been on the road for some time, appearing at cost price or below, we formed our own collectively run record label to promote ideas and to undermine the stranglehold that the major labels had both creatively and commercially over 'signed' (read 'captive') artists. Of the hundred or so artists that were released on our label, Crass Records, not one was 'signed', no paper-work was worked upon and no-one was expected to do anything but their best. The whole operation worked on trust and co-operation and without exception it was successful.

Selling records at under half the price of the majors, we demonstrated that huge profits were not necessary (unless you hankered after a Mercedes, a pad in California and needed to support a bad habit). The DIY ethic behind Crass was one which inspired untold numbers of activists. We weren't attempting to sell anything, we were seeking to share our ideas and any small profits that we might accumulate with as many like-minded people as possible. The limo-style exclusivity demonstrated by the so-called punk élite was an anathema to us: we were our own band, own roadies, own management, own PR and own label. The ideas that we promoted (pacifism, vegetarianism, anarchism, feminism, environmentalism, activism) were heartfelt and considered, and, like the Internet now, posed a major threat to established music business practises. No wonder then that we were lambasted by the lackey music press. No wonder that HMV banned our records or that the BBC black-listed them. No wonder that when our records were outselling any other band in the UK they did not appear in the charts.

Crass' effects will not be found within the confines of rock 'n' roll history (from which we have largely been written out), but in the genuinely autonomous movement that we inspired. Without Crass, punk would have died the death of all pop music fads; Rotten's was not a 'false' promise because it was no promise at all. Socially, The Pistols contributed nothing but loud-mouthed cynicism, whereas we succeeded in creating a meaningful political dialogue. That is our legacy, which is a long way from the regressive kitsch nostalgia of punk postcards for tourists, and the endless, pointless re-forming of bands who had nothing to say twenty-five years ago, and even less to say today. Which, conveniently, brings me round to this book, *Love Songs*.

When Mark from Pomona first contacted us regarding the book, I wasn't altogether convinced. We'd worked with Pomona before and I trusted their credentials, but much as I love Crass and every-thing that it stood for, in twenty-five years I've moved on. Did I really want to be Crass all over again? Punk was then, whereas this is now. My current work appears to be as unacceptable to the main-stream as Crass was then, so am I for ever fated to be dredging around in the past? On this reckoning, by the time any interest is shown in my latest novel I'll be six foot under, which might please the publisher's accountant, but won't be much use to me. It was these thoughts, plus the fact that I'd recently been almost killed by a recalcitrant squad car (not the Vice Squad) that led me to consider my 'body of work'. That might sound a bit grand, but I've been writing all my life and am I think justifiably proud of the work that I have produced. The anonymity of Crass had served a purpose which to my mind had outlived itself. Many years back I'd written the slogan *'there is no authority but yourself'*, now was the time to stand up and be counted. I wanted my work back. I wanted to be me, not Crass. So, having checked with the rest of the band that it was okay to break the code and put a name to our songs, I got back to Mark to give him the go ahead.

Now, having just proof-read the first draft of the book, I am reminded of just how serious a matter it was being Crass. From the Vice Squad to *Sounds*, MI5 to the British Movement, the KGB to a skinhead sending us classified information from the Falklands, the Pentagon to a prostitute who claimed she had photos of Dennis Thatcher giving her one up the kyhber, the IRA to the mother and child who were doing bank jobs to finance what remained of the Red Brigade, we got it from all sides. Tin Pan Alley? That was the least of our worries, and on top of all that there was the almost constant stream of lost visitors wanting to know if they had found Crass. It was pretty hard being some kind of living Holy Grail.

I recall one morning looking out of my bedroom window and seeing two very small but spikey heads bobbing around in the hedge that fronts the house. I decided to do nothing about it; if they could wait, so could I. Sometime towards evening I remembered them, and strolled round to the hedge. They were still there. I got closer and could hear them giggling, closer still and they froze. Eventually one of them mustered up the courage to ask the inevitable question: "Are you Crass?" We let them put up their tent at the bottom of the garden. They stayed for a week, playing our albums rather too loudly on a distorting ghetto-blaster while sewing together an incredibly beautiful Crass banner which, as a parting gift, they gave us. We displayed it at all subsequent gigs.

Re-reading the songs, I found that I could readily recall the atmosphere and the location in which they'd been created. *Banned From The Roxy* was written in Eve's garden before she moved in with us. Much of it was about our renowned gig at the fabled yet ill-fated Roxy, however, the line 'they just sit there on their over-fed arses living off the fat of less fortunate classes' was a direct reference to Eve's neighbours who on that sun-drenched afternoon were over-stretching the deckchairs in the meticulously laundered next-door garden. They were a particularly obnoxious couple, he a farm manager who was mean to cattle, and she a local do-gooder and gossip who was mean to people. Their main ambition in life appeared to be to have Eve evicted from her home, an ambition that a year or so later they brought to fruition. I suppose that in their aspiration towards buttoned-down respectability it is inevitable their bile should have risen against the ragged trousered philistines hanging around next door. Which is in no way to apologise for them. They were thoroughly nasty people and I'm glad that they're immortalised in my song.

Who Dunnit was written at our kitchen table, but it was inspired by the sunday lunches that I shared as a child with my family. Dad carved the meat and Mum served the pudding. It was all very ordered. The only time that I recall the brevity of the occasion being broken was when Tones, my older brother, asked for more custard. With a sly grin cast in my direction, he very, very slowly asked Mum to pass the cus ... turd. Neither Mum nor Dad were in the least bit amused, but my mirth was so uncontrollable that I was banished to my bedroom until I calmed down. Thirty years later, Tones' joke became the basis for a song which even the music press were unable to dismiss as 'too serious'. We did however receive a copy of the record sawn in half by an angry punk who informed us that he'd spent the last of his dole money on the offending article and that he didn't think it very funny. I thought it was a scream, but then I guess the angry punk had never spent Sunday lunch with my family.

So yes, for all the laughs, of which there were many, punk was a serious business, a force for change to which those who the media claimed were its founding fathers (The Pistols and The Clash) made no contribution whatsoever. A handful of second-rate shock 'n' roll records does not a revolution make, but look no further than Seattle and Genoa to see that a sincere and informed attack on the status quo could.

'*I'm so bored with the USA*'? Then why snort coke in the beast's belly? '*I am an anarchist*'? Then why not act like one rather than like a capitalist goon?

In an ill-conceived attempt to get Crass onto his books, the manager of Sham 69, and later, Boy George, once informed us without a hint of irony that he could "market revolution", by which he of course meant that he saw us and our message of personal autonomy as a commodity. We told him in no uncertain terms what he could do with his pig-ignorance.

It was The Pistols' and the Clash's willing acceptance of commodification that should exclude them from any serious discussion on the subject of the 'movement' for which punk is best remembered. If however it's simply a trip down memory lane that you're after, throw away this book, forget the very crucial issues of a world choking from American moral and military terrorism, and pop out to Woolies for a cut-price CD of *Punk As It Really Was*, and while you're about it, grab a six-pack so you can piss yourself into oblivion.

In a rampantly capitalist society dominated by the sickeningly Orwellian spin of Big Brother Bush and his arse-licking paramour, Tony Blair, it comes as no real surprise that dimbos like Johnny Rotten should be allotted space in the history books; ignorance is, after all, strength. In challenging that ignorance, Crass inspired what was perhaps one of the most powerful cultural movements of the late twentieth century, the radical substance of which is as alive today as it was then. In the fearsome wake of the jingoistic clap-trap generated by the WTC, our messages are as pointed now as they were prophetic twenty-five years ago.

Before Crass, the punk 'movement' consisted of a small crowd of fashion-conscious, self-important rock 'n' roll hacks whose interest in global politics extended little further than the Kings Road catwalk which they inhabited. The Pistols had no true political agenda, very limited political awareness and no programme at all beyond self-ingratiation and profit. Punk as it was promoted by its key entrepreneurs and by the hack music press was no more than another tired scam exploiting youthful energy; just another case of cash for crap. The Pistols were no more than the Spice Girls of their day.

In conclusion, you might very well be asking what in hell this has got to do with love. The answer is simple—everything. Despite what Hollywood and Tin Pan Alley might want us to believe, love is not an emotional commodity exclusively reserved for a personal possession (wife, husband, partner, lover), neither is it the gift of a diamond. Real love is the fight to free the slaves who in their degrading poverty are forced to dig those 'precious' stones from the earth. Love is not a puppy for Christmas. Real love is the fight to free animals from the obscene torture of the vivisector's scalpel and the butcher's knife. Love then is not a word, it is total action. Rather than being 'in a state', love is a state of being.

For as long as there are those who use their lives to devalue that of others, it is up to those who love life to oppose them. That is the only true meaning I can give the word. So here they are, 'Love Songs'. I hope they inspire you to act.

Penny Rimbaud
August 2003

ACTS OF LOVE

PENNY RIMBAUD

I've seen so many dreams washed away in tears,
now, dry eyed, do I see any clearer?

I

When you woke this morning you looked so rocky-eyed,
blue and white normally, but strange ringed like that in black.
It doesn't get much better,
your voice can get just ripped up shouting in vain.
Maybe someone hears what you say,
but you're still on your own at night.
You've got to make such a noise to understand the silence,
screaming like a jackass, ringing ears so you can't hear the silence,
even when it's there, like the wind seen from the window,
seeing it but not being touched by it.

1984

I would sleep,
my body would exercise.

I shall sleep
and deny it exercise.

My body will fuse with sheets,
my mind will fuse with night air.

Take care not to disturb them,
they sleep. Should you disturb them,
BEWARE.

They will not both awake.
You will face the animal or the essence.

1984

3

It is no time since the open sky,
the clouds,
the rain.

I am here, as proud as yesterday.

Who am I?
Can I recall this name of mine?
Did I yesterday?

The yellow soil can hold me now.

Oh that I could lose the mind that shapes this body.

1984

4

My mind tumbles in a fountain of sound.

Keen to be caught by each note,
I jump and chop and change.

At each point I am lost.

I throw all aside, exhausted.

1984

5

Hold my eyes,
they are heavy.
I sigh.

The vast sound bursts across the room,
blazing colour within the space I cannot see.
I hear voices in the space.
I float in the dry sounds.

My body turns and shakes in the sounds,
my being floats away, across the space,
with the sounds.

1984

6

Into tunnels I run.

Confounded by the water I dive.

I swim.

Roach, carp, bream, jump in the hurtling waters.

Trout.

I'm thrown onto the gravel shore,
dried by the sun,
the wind.

1984

7

Who frets tonight to see me tomorrow,
or next week?

The excitement.

Can the grass wait for my feet tomorrow?
What am I to be tonight?

Will dragons come?

1984

8

The walks in muddy soils,
the black skies,
the bush,
this tree.

I've seen a great number of species,
I've seen the grass snow covered,
I've seen footprints following me.
Are you behind me?

1984

9

I sing,
surely I live?
The violets are bursting on every hedgerow.

I shout,
hands at an angle from my mouth,
to act as an amplifier.

I have never out-shouted the wind.
Where the reward?

Good day.   Hearsay.
Walk with me to the apple orchard.
We shall sit there until the blossoms fall.

1984

The dusk of my hours await;
I must leave you now.

I have waited on you;
I must return.

You have not spoken.

I walk to the pale mountains of my soul.

I shall not return.
Vermilion cloaks hide my bodies.

1984

.

Veiled by evening gloom,
they make me animate.
They rest, become static.

We have such demands on each other.

1984

I say goodbye to you,
I gentle caress my own hand as if it was yours.

See the ground open up for me?
Will you not save me?
HOW THEN?

NO HOW.
Perversity drives, drives me from you.

1984

I have walked enough,

I've paced behind you like a third leg.

You are not aware that I have paced behind.

1984

Yesterday I laughed with you.

Yesterday the song of the earth rang in my ears.
Sweet fool, listen. You can hear the song of the earth.

1984

Empty heads,
swaying from tears to smiles.

Void in frosty mornings.
Twig,
grass,
flower,
boil on barren soil.

Morning,
our eternal sorrow awakes us in our beds.

We are caught by the senses,
sense to senseless.

1984

Illusion,
speak from beneath the black vacuum that is your form.

Evening,
we wait.
Tireless movement all around.
We do not move.
Arms shake towards some hidden deity.
We are motionless,
tense,
waiting.

Can you hear me this windy night?
Do you hear me above the tearing of the trees?

You are not listening this night,
yet I shall speak all the same.

By no chance will you hear;
the wind carries my voice above and beyond.

1984

Where have we smiled like this before,
clapsed each others hands?

Was it you that cried, choking, when first the blackbirds sang?

My worst moments are destroyed in the gleam of your eye.

1984

Whilst walking, I have often passed you.
Now our walking is our oneness.

You are not alone,
lost in your own dreams and desires.

Alone we are together,
together we are as one.

1984

Those hours are distant shadows.
Silent,
the beating sea
throwing winds upon a distant shore.
Beneath the silence that holds us apart is a name.
The name seizes its own reality.

Where were you then?
Hiding in prosperous groves of lemon and grape?
You push aside the ivy with your white fingers.
I shall never forget you.
The silence of those fingers blinds my eyes,
my ears are blinded by the whiteness.

Walk here, here and beyond.
Wait for me by the naked sand.
The waves roll contented to the sea.
Hold me as a memory.
I'm a huge whale that fights for oceans and air.

1984

In the cell that is ours there is no pity,
no sunrise on the cold plain that is our soul,
no beckoning to a warm horizon.

All beauty eludes us, and we wait.

1984.

The blinking of an eye,
the snapping of a finger,
are all things.

All things exist the second before we consider them.

1984

In my attachment to infinity I have no definition.

All things are solid.

There is no space in which to relate.

1984

One foot before the other I walk,
always mindful.

Travelling nowhere,
I am always surrounded.

I stop and find that I have moved,
move and find that I have stopped.

One foot before the other.

1984

I walk with no knowledge of myself,
move and all things are carried with me.

I cannot be separated.

Where then do I exist?

Moments before the identity you have of me.

The illusion of past realities,
the dawn breaking in the windless sky.

The cockerel crows.

All things are reawoken.
They continue their path in silence.

1984

Wait.
I shall see you through this illusion.

Balance sea mists,
desert suns,
raving dogs,
she cats,
burning fire,
violent flame,
poisonous waters.

I shall see you through this illusion.

In seeing this, my senses will devour it.
Devoured it will be fluid in my being,
one within our oneness.

Balance all things on the wall of lies that they may be destroyed.
Place all things beneath the mill and wait.
They are destroyed in our understanding of them.

I have found peace,
I have heard waves,
seen the wind pull mightier forms than mine back
to the soil from which they came.

I was driven to the wall of lies, hoping to find solace.
There is no real love in the paradise of the senses.
All is thrown away by the wall of lies.

Let there be peace.

I shall see through this illusion.

1984

Soft grass,
green grass, better not stand here,
because the grass will be turning brown.

Blue sky,
soft sky, better not stand here,
because the rain will come tumbling down.

Everything changes, moment by moment,
caught within its own game.

You can't live avoiding the insects in the path.
You can't tip-toe through forests pretending that you've never
been there.

Everywhere you go you bend the earth,
you can't feel guilty.
Everywhere you sleep you warm the earth,
you mustn't feel guilty.

Frog, toad, newt, salmon, all cold water-beings, bed in my tears.
Butterfly, bird, bee, moth, all flying-beings, bed in my hair.
Cat, cow, goat, dog, all warm flesh-beings, bed in our arms.

In your time I live.
When you awake, I shall awake.

Let us live together, we could love each other.

Now I walk.
No dreams of yesterday.

Not one path I don't already know.

This way and that,
that way and this.

The grass grows, it meets me.
The wind blows, it meets me.

No dreams of yesterday.

Journeys are nothing but reflections in a static pool.

1984

There was a window through which I watched a cherry grow.
Each day there was a change.

Frail pink blossom in the pale blue sky.
The budding leaves.
Hard green berries hung central in the window.

In August a child snatched the ripened berry from the tree.

Each day I watch the space that is left.

1984

The warm patch where once my body lay is still there.

I am both here and there.

1984

The naked brow frets in the cold,
wrinkled against itself.
No silence in its illusion.
No dream to calm the head.

No cold. No fear.

1984

Hilltops.
Mountains hidden in mist grey sky.

No lark climbs into the azure sky.
No nest is left cold.
Every branch bends in the wind.
Every wave finds a coastline.
Morning is morning,
I share it with all things,
by myself.

I am challenged,
by myself.

I share it with all things.
By myself I am everything.

1984

33

The season has us confused,
we are the straggle headed,
nodding in the sun.
In a universe of thought there is no dream,
no sound that has not already been made.

If you sing out of confusion you add to it.

Be silent as the gentle movement of the hours,
reflect that within and without it will gameful run its course.
No one can stop that.

You inherit nothing.
The guilt you feel is your own.

Try and give your pain to the swaying field of barley-corn;
it will sway to your tears.
It will draw your tears as water from the soil
with which to strengthen its own growth.

1984

A stone is margined by its own shadow.
A cockerel crows.

Feet, caressed by kitten tongues, touch stone floors.
Winds scratch and bounce on slated roofs.

The grass is wet. Raindrops run down each blade to the earth.
Clay turns darker, damper, grabs at passing toes.

The song of thrush,
starling,
robin,
sparrow,
blackbird,
ring-dove and wren catches the wind and runs,
parallel through time.

Each sound is held static in the solidity of space.

Each moment the day grows wider in its possibilities.

1984

This morning there is shelter,
my journey is fast.

If this morning is a sad song, sing on,
sad song, don't mind, sing on,
keep on, don't mind, sing on.

If all the world was as gentle as the breeze within my hands,
if all the days weren't numbered for those souls
who walk aimless down the high-road,
if the space between us was as solid as I see it for you all,
sober thought,
there'd be no sad song.

1984

Cross the barley-grain, walk beneath the elm and the beech,
the oak.

If all this was our world,
not mine, not yours,
if all this was our world,
one we'd be, can you see?
Old song.
If you open up your heart just a little, you can whisper.

Old song.

36

I'm glad that the sun has awoken me again.
I live still.

Each new day I live again.
What more?

1984

It's you who makes the world around you.
The silence is yours.

In every line upon your face
and every fold that holds your eyes,
a story.
That story is you.

There is no cosmetic for our frustrations.

If upon my tears you build the utopia of which you dream,
be warned,
your petty prejudice will push you again into maliciousness.

Beyond our alienation
and its tiresome manifestations
of violence and greed,
there is balance and harmony.

Isn't the world already at peace?

I suggest togetherness, proclaiming my love and compassion.
Will you make that into commodity, asset and possession?
It's you who makes the world around you,
you alone can answer for it.

1984

You ask for the world,
it is yours.
Your confusion is the box in which you put answers,
your limitations are the walls of the box.

Destroy the box.

There are no lights to guide your path, only your love.
If you show your love, there are no questions,
no beginning and no end,
you stand apart from your confusions,
your achievements
and spent realities.

1984

The beautiful eyes of the warrior,
they are nothing but boot polish.

1984

40

The fox runs to the east,
beech trees line the field.

How strange. The fox runs against the sun.

The wind changes direction,
the tides come and go.
We wake, we eat, we sleep.

How confusing. Nothing appears as it truly is.

1984

A thousand separate winds blow.
The boat on the lake is lost in the confusion.

How lucky that we can rely on the singular purpose of nature.

1984

The changing seasons,
the changing winds.
In Spring the snow melts upon the mountains,
the streams run thickly.

How tiresomely solid we seem.

1984

The tree bends in the wind.
We too bend to externals.

Beware, the tree has no idea of itself.

1984

How fortunate that we have no branch on our body
from which to shake leaves in Spring.

1984

Running we breathe deeply.
Resting we breathe softly.

How my head aches as I chop wood.

1984

The horseless rider dreams of sleep.

The horse runs weightless.

1984

Crossing the road I am unaware of the cars.

A man sat in the snow beneath a mighty oak, reflecting upon his doubts.

In Spring, the tree budded.
The man reflected upon his confusions.

In Summer, the tree gave shade to the man. He reflected upon his agonies.

In Autumn, the man was showered with leaves.

1984

Your clumsy head.

HOW IT BOUNCES.

Acts of Love was written during the late-Sixties and early-Seventies and released as a recording in 1984 to, in Penny Rimbaud's words, *'demonstrate that the source of my anger was love rather than hate...'*

REALITY ASYLUM

PENNY RIMBAUD

I AM NO FEEBLE
Christ / Not me / He
hangs in glib delight upon
his cross / Above my body /
Lowly me / Christ forgive
/ forgive? / Holy He / He
holy / He holy? / Shit He
forgives / Forgive? Forgive? / I? I? Me? I? I vomit for you Jesu /
Christy Christus / Puke upon your papal throne / Wrapped you are
in the bloody shroud of churlish suicide / Wrapped I am in the
muddy cloud of hellish genocide / Petulant child / I have suffered
for you / Where you have never known me / I too must die / Will
you be shadowed in the arrogance of my death? Your valley truth
/ What lights pass those
pious heights? / What
passing bells for these in
their trucks? / For you /
Lord / You are the flag-
bearer of these nations /
One against the other that
die in the mud / No piety /
No deity / Is that your forgiveness? / Saint / Martyr /
Goat / Billy / Forgive? /
Shit He forgives / He
hangs upon his cross in
self-righteous judgement /
Hangs in crucified delight
/ Nailed to the extent of

1979

[51]

His vision / His cross / His
manhood / His violence.
Guilt / Sin / He would nail
my body to his cross / As if
I might have waited upon
him in the garden / As if I
might have perfumed His
body / washed those bloody feet / This woman that He seeks /
Suicide visionary / Death reveller / Rake / Rapist / Gravedigger /
Earthmover / Lifefucker / Jesu / You scooped the pits of Auschwitz /
The soil of Treblinka is rich in your guilt / the sorrow of your
tradition / Your stupid humility is the crown of thorns we all must
wear / For you / Ha / Master / Master of gore / Enigma / Stigma /
Stigmata / Errata / Eraser
/ The cross is the mast of
your oppression / You fly
there / vain flag / You
carry it / Wear it on your
back / Lord / Your back /
Enola is your gaiety /
Suffer little children to
come unto me / Suffer in
that horror / Hirohorror /
Hirrohiro / Hiroshimmer /
Shimmerhiro / Hiroshima
/ Hiroshima / The bodies
are your delight / The
incandescent flame is the
spirit of it / They come to

1979

[52]

you / Jesu / To you / The
nails are the only trinity /
Hold them in your
corpsey gracelessness /
The image that I have had
to suffer / These nails at
my temple / The cross is
the virgin body of womanhood that you defile / In your guilt you
turn your back / Nailed to that body / Lame-arse Jesus calls me
sister / There are no words for my contempt / Every woman is a
cross in his filthy theology / He turns His back on me in His fear / His
vain delight is the pain I bear / Alone He hangs / His choice / His
choice / Alone / Alone / His voice / His voice / He shares nothing / This
Christ / Sterile / Impotent /
Fucklove prophet of death
/ He is the ultimate pornography / He / He / Hear
us / Jesus / You sigh alone
in your cockfear / You lie
alone in your womanfear /
You die alone in your man
fear / Alone / Jesu / Alone /
In your cockfear / Cunt-
fear / Womanfear / Man-
fear / Alone in your fear /
Alone in your fear / Your
fear / Your fear / Warfare /
Warfare / Jesus died for
his own sins / Not mine.

1979

WHERE NEXT COLUMBUS?

EVE LIBERTINE

ANOTHER'S HOPE ANOTHER'S GAME
Another's loss   another's gain
Another's lies   another's truth
Another's doubt   another's proof

Another's left   another's right
Another's peace   another's fight
Another's name   another's aim
Another's fall   another's fame

Another's pride   another's shame
Another's love   another's pain
Another's hope   another's game
Another's loss   another's gain.

Another's lies   another's truth
Another's doubt   another's proof
Another's left   another's right
Another's peace   another's fight

Marx had an idea from the confusion of his head,
then there were a thousand more waiting to be led.
The books are sold, the quotes are bought,
you learn them well and then you're caught.

Another's left   another's right
Another's peace   another's fight

1981

Mussolini had an idea from the confusion of his heart,
then there were a thousand more waiting to play their part.
The stage was set, the costumes worn,
and another empire of destruction born.

Another's name   another's aim
Another's fall   another's fame

Jung had an idea from the confusion of his dream,
then there were a thousand more waiting to be seen.
You're not yourself, the theory says,
but I can help, your complex pays.

Another's hope   another's game
Another's loss   another's gain

1981

Sartre had an idea from the confusion of his brain,
then there were a thousand more indulging in his pain,
revelling in isolation and existential choice;
how can you be alone if you use another's voice?

Another's lies   another's truth
Another's doubt   another's proof

The idea born in someone's mind,
is nurtured by a thousand blind.
Anonymous beings, vacuous souls,
do you fear the confusion, your lack of control?
You lift your arm to write a name,
so caught up in the identity game.

Who do you see?   Who do you watch?
Who's your leader? Which is your flock?
Who do you watch? Who do you watch?
Who's your leader? Which is your flock?

Einstein had an idea from the confusion of his knowledge,
then there were a thousand more turning it to advantage.
They realised that their god was dead,
so they reclaimed power with the bomb instead.

Another's code   another's brain
They'll shower us all in deadly rain.

Jesus had an idea from the confusion of his soul,
then there were a thousand more waiting to take control.
The guilt is sold, forgiveness bought,
the cross is there as your reward.

Another's love   another's pain
Another's pride   another's shame

Do you watch from a distance from the side you have chosen?
Whose answers serve you best? Who'll save you from confusion?
Who will leave you an exit and a comfortable cover?
Who will take you to the edge, but never drop you over?

1981

BIG A LITTLE A

PENNY RIMBAUD

BIG A LITTLE A BOUNCING B,
the system might have got you, but it won't get me.
One, two, three, four . . .

External control, are you gonna let them get you?
Do you wanna be a prisoner in the boundaries they set you?
You say you want to be yourself,
by Christ do you think they'll let you?
They're out to get you get you get you get you get you get you . . .

Hello, hello, hello, this is the Lord God, can you hear?
Hellfire and damnation's what I've got for you down there.
On earth I have ambassadors: archbishop, vicar, Pope.
We'll blind you with morality, you'd best abandon any hope.
We're telling you you'd better pray 'cos you were born in sin,
right from the start we'll build a cell and then we'll lock you in.
We sit in holy judgement condemning those that stray,
we offer our forgiveness, but first we'll make you pay.

External control, are you gonna let them get you?
Do you wanna be a prisoner in the boundaries they set you?
You say you want to be yourself,
by Christ do you think they'll let you?
They're out to get you get you get you get you get you get you . . .

1980

Hello, hello, hello; now here's a message from your Queen,
as figurehead of the status quo I set the social scene.
I'm most concerned about my people, want to give them peace,
so I'm making sure they stay in line with my army and police.
My prisons and my mental homes have ever open doors
for those amongst my subjects who dare to ask for more.
Unruliness and disrespect are things I can't allow,
so I'll see the peasants grovel if they refuse to bow.

External control, are you gonna let them get you?
Do you wanna be a prisoner in the boundaries they set you?
You say you want to be yourself,
by Christ do you think they'll let you?
They're out to get you get you get you get you get you get you …

Introducing the Prime Sinister, she's a mother to us all,
like the dutch boy's finger in the dyke her arse is in the wall.
Holding back the future, waiting for the seas to part,
if Moses did it with his faith, she'll do it with an army
who at times of threatened crisis are certain to be there,
guarding national heritage no matter what or where.
Palaces for kings and queens, mansions for the rich,
protection for the wealthy, defence of privilege;
they've learnt the ropes in Ireland, engaged in civil war,
fighting for the ruling classes in their battle against the poor.
So Ireland's just an island? It's an island of the mind.
Great Britain? Future? Bollocks, you'd better look behind.
Round every other corner stands P.C. 1984,
guardian of the future, he'll implement the law.
He's there as a grim reminder that no matter what you do,
Big Brother's system's always there with his beady eyes on you.

From God to local bobby, in home and street and school,
they've got your name and number, while you've just got their rule.
We've got to look for methods to undermine those powers,
it's time to change the tables, the future must be ours.

Be exactly who you want to be, do what you want to do,
I am he and she is she but you're the only you.
No one else has got your eyes, can see the things you see,
it's up to you to change your life, and my life's up to me.
The problems that you suffer from are problems that you make,
the shit we have to climb through is the shit we choose to take.
If you don't like the life you live, change it now, it's yours,
nothing has effect if you don't recognise the cause.
If the programme's not the one you want, get up, turn off the set,
it's only you who can decide what life you're gonna get.
If you don't like religion you can be the antichrist,
if you're tired of politics you can be an anarchist.
But no one ever changed the church by pulling down a steeple,
and you'll never change the system by bombing Number Ten.
Systems just aren't made of bricks, they're mostly made of people,
you may send them into hiding, but they'll be back again.
If you don't like the rules they make, refuse to play their game,
if you don't want to be a number, don't give them your name.
If you don't want to be caught out, refuse to hear their question,
silence is a virtue, use it for your own protection.
They'll try to make you play their game, refuse to show your face,
if you don't want to be beaten down, refuse to join their race.
Be exactly who you want to be, do what you want to do,
I am he and she is she, but you're the only you.

1980

A MESSAGE TO THATCHER,
HER GOVERNMENT, THOSE WHO SUPPORT HER
AND ALL THOSE WHO ARE WILLING TO SEND LAMBS
TO THE SLAUGHTERHOUSE OF WAR

PENNY RIMBAUD

WE NEVER ASKED FOR WAR, NOR IN THE INNOCENCE OF our birth were we aware of it. We never asked for war, nor in the struggle to realisation did we feel that there was a need for it. We never asked for war, nor in the joyful colours of our childhood were we conscious of its darkness.

. . .

The sky is empty and it's turning different shades of colour,
*   it never did before and we never asked for war.*
My mind is empty and my body different shades of torture,
*   it never was before and we never asked for war.*
The buildings are empty and the countryside is wasteland,
*   it never was before and we never asked for war.*
The playgrounds are empty and the children limbless corpses,
*   they never were before and they never asked for war.*
No-one is moving and no doves fly here.
No-one is thinking and no doves fly here.
No-one remembers beyond all this fear.
No doves fly here.

– The Mob, 1982

. . .

1983

We never asked for war; this glib, horrific indifference, that leads young men barely old enough to have experienced anything of the joy of life to kill and be killed, is something that you have imposed upon us. You snatch these young bodies from the brain-washing cradle of the schoolroom to be maimed, mutilated and slaughtered in the cold grave of your cynicism. You tear these young bodies from their homes to die in the foreign soil of your barren, bloodstained minds. How perverted you are, how distorted and twisted, how divorced from the simple joy of existence. You dare to threaten the one life that we have with your pained violence. In the crystal light of our lives, you are the darkest shadow.

Each body that you shovel into the mass graves of history is another darling boy that you have bled, another precious life that you have defiled, another act of creation that you have dared to violate. What is birth to you but another rag that you may wring and slap and beat and discard? What is life to you but another plastic body-bag into which you defecate? What is death to you but the disfigured bodies of our children upon whose angel faces you smear your rancid droppings?

How grand you must feel as you chart out your battlefields; each feature on that map describes the desolation of your mind. How powerful you must feel as you order the plunder and rape of those battlefields; each bayonet that turns in some contracting stomach is the pointing finger of your right hand. How omnipotent you must feel as those young men stumble in the death of those battlefields; each death is part of you that dies.

How glorious war. How rich the experience of war.

Those castaway boys, deranged, dismembered, crying, homeless, are the reality of your horror, the actuality of your insanity. That horror is the heritage that you create. That insanity is the tradition that you leave to those as yet unborn. The frightened corpses of the living are shadowed by your arrogance. The limbless corpses of the dead are devoured in your lust for power. The maggots that inch away at the rotting flesh are your true compatriots. You keep them fed, they are your true companions. Those bodies were my brothers that you have destroyed. That battlefield is my home that you have burnt in your fire.

Your minds are filth. Your lives are corruption. You are the walking dead, the parasites who bleed this earth of ours, that dry the waters from the river-beds and give us blood in its place.

      .   .   .

YOU STAND ACCUSED OF PREMEDITATED, CALCULATED AND COLD-BLOODED MURDER. YOUR CRIMES ARE WELL DOCUMENTED. YOUR GUILT IS THE RESPONSIBILITY THAT ONE DAY YOU WILL HAVE TO REALISE.

Crass, 3rd June 1983

1983

YES, SIR, I WILL

PENNY RIMBAUD

The door stands open—
Across lines, invisible hands are held,
golden streamers building in the night.
Alone, the possibilities are enormous.
Step outside and parasites, deprived of their meat,
wait to suck on tiring flesh.
Unending statistics that fatten leaders, prisoners of their morality.
Afraid of death, we can not save ourselves.
To breathe is not enough.

— Gee Vaucher

1983

. . .

WHEN YOU WOKE THIS MORNING YOU LOOKED SO ROCKY-EYED,
blue and white normally, but strange ringed like that in black.
It doesn't get much better,
    your voice can get just ripped up shouting in vain.
Maybe someone hears what you say,
    but you're still on your own at night.
You've got to make such a noise to understand the silence,
screaming like a jackass, ringing ears so you can't hear the silence,
even when it's there, like the wind seen from the window,
seeing it but not being touched by it.

Words sometimes don't seem to mean much;
of anyone we've used more that most,
feelings from the heart that have been distorted and mocked,
thrown around in the spectacle, the grand social circus.

Up against the rows of grey robots who control our lives
the things we have to offer sometimes seem so frail.
As they plan destruction and gain respectability,
we offer our creativity and are made outcasts.

We didn't expect to find ourselves playing this part,
we were concerned with ideas, not rock and roll,
but we can't avoid that arena,
it's become a part of us even if we don't understand it.

In attempts to moderate, they ask why we don't write love songs.
What is it that we sing then?
Our love of life is total, everything we do is an expression of that.
Everything that we write is a love song.

We look for alternatives,
but the enormous power of the media makes it so difficult
to establish foundations.
Their lies and distortions are so extreme
that everything becomes poisoned and corrupted.
We can become media personalities,
but it is always on their terms.
We're tired of living up to other people's expectations
when our own are so much higher.
Intelligence seems so easily dismissed
when it doesn't conform to mainstream values.

1983

Lennon said "they hate you if you're clever and they despise a fool".
He was right.
Social intelligence merely requires agreement and compromise.
The boundaries are becoming narrower
        as the State becomes more paranoid.
Under authoritarian rule, conformity becomes the only security.
Fear is a powerful weapon against human development.
Cowering in our temples of self there's little chance of change;
the State is aware of that. The bomb serves many functions.
If fear of the omnipotent God is no more,
the nuclear Father will govern with his shepherd's crook,
drawing his flock closer to the valley of the shadow of death.

Those of us who stand out against the status quo
do so against all odds.
We cling so closely together
because we have little other than ourselves.

1983

Critics say that it's just punk rock or that we're just
        naïve anarchists.
They hope to discredit us with their labels and definitions.
Throughout history societies have condemned those who are later
        celebrated as heroes.
In so many bourgeois homes Van Gogh's sunflowers radiate
        from the walls,
yet he lived in utter misery, condemned by those very same people.
Why is it that the kind and gentle are subjected to violence
        and ridicule?
How is it that the small and mealy-minded have gained
        so much power?
What perversion has taken place that we are governed by fools?

We've had problems from self-appointed Gods,
    from bishops to MPs.
They've tried to ban our records
saying that we're a threat to decent society.
Fuck them. I hope we are.
What kind of depraved idiot thinks they can silence others by
    denying them their voice?
For fuck's sake, who are these lobotomists?
As if walls only had one side.
Whispered intimacies might not get through,
but cries of anguish know no barriers.
But how long do we shout for?
Denied the airwaves, we trust in the wind to carry what we say.
But sometimes we've found ourselves shouting into the wind
when we should have been confiding in each other.
It seems so absurd that we are denied the chance
    of ever being truly free.
The terrible inequalities of the peoples of this earth
make freedom at best a dream, at worst an insulting privilege.
What space is there for self-expression and personal development
when over half the world's population is starving?
There are so many things that might have been done,
but rooted on this spot in the desire to find solution,
there's little to see and feel
but the sighing and dying
of our world.
But for suffering
we might have been a part of it rather than apart from it.

1983

. . .

Making the compromises,
              what did you know? What did you care?
Brave fronts, deceitful disguises,
              what did you know? What did you care?
Turning a blind eye to the lies just to keep it all together,
but sometimes when I'm alone like this
       I wonder whether it's worth it.

Smiling and socialising,
              what did you know? What did you care?
Endless philosophising,
              what did you know? What did you care?
Surface agreements, statements of fact,
       trying to prove we can do it,
but sometimes when I'm alone like this
       I wonder who can see through it.

1983

Bargains and sacrifices,
              what did you know? What did you care?
Cheap tricks, cheaper devices,
              what did you know? What did you care?
Holding the vision, but losing our sight,
endlessly searching solution,
but sometimes when I'm alone like this
I wonder how much it's just institution.

              What did you know? What did you care?
Anarchy's become another word for 'got 10p to spare?'
              What did you know? What did you care?
Another way of saying 'I'm OK, sod you out there'.

Another token tantrum to cover up the fear.
                    What did you know? What did you care?
Another institution another cross to bear.
                    What did you know? What did you care?

. . .

Anything and everything can be so easily institutionalised,
a poor parody of itself, itself contained by itself.
There's no point in just mouthing the words.
The token tantrums just aren't enough,
nor is speed and weed and the Positive Creed;
exclusive clubs where the various tribes congratulate each other
        for doing fuck all
will achieve nothing but the strengthening of the status quo.
Punk has spawned another rock and roll élite,
cheap Rotten Vicious imitations thinking they'll change
        their world
with dyed hair and predictable gestures. Nouveau wankers.
There's a thousand empty stages waiting for their
        empty performances,
a thousand empty faces waiting for their empty stances.
How many times must we bear rehashed versions of
        Feeding Of The 5000
By jerks whose only fuck off to the system has been one
        off the wrist?
It's the *Feeding Of The 5 Knuckle Shuffle*...

1983

. . .

If there was no government, wouldn't there be chaos,
everybody running round, setting petrol bombs off?
And if there was no police force, tell me what you'd do
if thirty thousand rioters came running after you?
And who would clean the sewers? Who'd mend my television?
Wouldn't people lay about without some supervision?
Who'd drive the fire engines? Who'd fix my video?
If there were no prisons, well, where would robbers go?

And what if I told you to Fuck Off?

What if there's no army to stop a big invasion?
Who'd clean the bogs and sweep the floors?
    We'd have all immigration.
Who'd pull the pint at the local pub?
    Where'd I get my fags?
Who'd empty out my dustbins?
    Would I still get plastic bags?
If there were no hospitals, and no doctors too,
if I'd broken both my legs, where would I run to?
If there's no medication, if there were no nurses,
wouldn't people die a lot? And who would drive the hearses?

And what if I told you to Fuck Off?

If there were no butchers shops, what would people eat?
You'd have everybody starving if they didn't eat their meat.
If there was no water, what would people drink?
Who'd flush away the you-know-what?
    But of course MINE never stink.
What about the children?
    Who'd teach them in the schools?

Who'd make the beggers keep in line?
    Learn them all the rules?
Who'd tell us whitewash windows?
    When to take down doors?
Tell us make a flask of tea and survive the holocaust?

– Steve Ignorant

. . .

The rock and roll swindler says it's OK to plunder,
so the pirates set sail to rape any ethnic culture
        they can plug a mike to.
The imperialists rub their hands in glee
as the slave-boy hunts out butt-ends in the garbage cans.
Is it any wonder there was such sickening celebration
        over the Task Force
when so called radicals work hand in hand with the ruling élite?
Yesterday those wily creeps rejected the status quo,
today they smarm and charm passageways to its very heart.
Where's the free individual in all that?
Where's the hope and aspiration?
Identities have become corporations,
social egos and media moulds,
scholars of ad-man's dreams. Prescribed futures;
must we all down aspirins and shine beneath borrowed tans?
Are we really so dumb, so cowered into submission
that not only are we prepared to eat shit,
we're also prepared to say thanks for the privilege?
Why should we accept servility as a bargain for dignity?
Why should we passively accept death as a bargain for living?
Why accept this robbery of life? Why accept this pillage?

1983

For Christ's sake take up your bed and walk.
Let the blind see and the deaf hear.
The rights of the individual are dependent upon
you realising your right as an individual.
People are so easily deluded
　　　into thinking they've instrumented choice
where in reality they're nothing but passive observers.
Passive observers do nothing but passively observe,
passively soak up creativity and say 'Wow, that's me',
passively soak up destruction and say 'Oh no, not us, not me'.
There are those who strive for value and meaning,
who search for reason and purpose;
their efforts are negated by the passive observers.

They spend days before the TV set so burned out,
is it any wonder they've lost all sense of vision and possibility?
What chance does anyone have when all the spaces are filled,
sipping breakfast teas to the sound of Space Invaders?

Television is today's Nuremberg.
Bowing to its authority, they become it.
I've seen four-year-old children conforming to media roles,
mainlining the gross theatre that will become their lives.
The television has so dampened people's anger.
The population is mesmerised by the flickering screen,
and the streets, where the politics of reality were once created,
are deserted at night and the rulers sleep secure.
They are under no threat as long as the people are sedated.
Those who suffer headaches from excessive intake of electrons
　　　are prescribed valium,
or pay for a fix at the pub where men have to piss up the wall
and the stench of urine lasts well into the next pint.

Entertainment is designed to gloss over real problems,
and very often those who profess dissent
        only add to the deception.
Words are banded about,
        but always at the whim of the puppeteer.
Actionless sloganeering is just another Punch and Judy show.

Any information that we receive concerning the real world
        is carefully controlled.
Why else would fiction have such license?
We are allowed to see endless theatrical deaths,
but when the real deaths started on the Falklands,
Government censors prevented us from seeing them.
We were given the excuse of 'National Security'
by the lying shits who were interested only
        in saving their political skins.
It didn't matter a fuck to them how many died
as long as their popularity ratings didn't suffer,
for that reason alone we were shielded from the truth.
While the real violence is kept from us,
we are exposed to constant pantomimes of death and destruction.
Those in power are rightly aware that if we had access
        to the real facts
we would cease to be simply passive observers.
Media coverage of Vietnam created massive dissent in the USA.
Thatcher's government was aware of that when,
        embarking on the Falklands charade,
they refused press cards to anyone who they knew
        would not support their line.
Those who did travel to the Falklands found their
        reports dramatically cut down.

Meanwhile, at home, we were fed fabrications
	of Britain's 'glorious war'.
The truth that is now filtering out paints a very
	different picture.

It's often been said that truth is the first casualty of war,
it is, but the same could be said of life.
From birth we are threatened and beaten into submission
by family, church, school and State.
From then on we're easy game for the powermongers.
Like pathetic circus dogs we hunt out praise
or, when our true nature finds its way to the surface,
we hide in the darkness, our tails between our legs.
At all costs we are prevented from realising our own potential.
We are conditioned into being passive observers.
If the ring-master offers war,
we have been conditioned to passively accept it.
War can only exist through passive acceptance.
It is nothing but a demonstration of the weakness of human will.
If the clown offered peace,
we will have been conditioned to accept that too,
but peace can not and will not be maintained
	through passive acceptance.
Peace will require constant demonstrations of personal strength,
constant effort, constant hard work,
reappraisal, consideration and devotion.
Which of those qualities were you taught in the schoolroom?
Whereas war simply requires the masses as cannon-fodder,
peace requires individuals to realise their own potential.
The odds are hopelessly against because the State deliberately
	destroys human will.

1983

Passive observers offer nothing but decay.
The flowerbeds need weeding,
        the roses need cutting back before winter.
Freed from sedation, released from bondage,
people would demonstrate their own strength,
but the powerful élite are aware of this
and already have tabs on those who they regard as subversives.
It is easy for them to single out and intimidate us,
and easier still for us simply not to bother.

.   .   .

It is impossible to gauge the effect that demands for peace
        may be having;
the authorities are skilled at concealing dissatisfaction.
For so long people have been saying 'no more war',
but for all those demands little has changed.
Seeing that the Peace Movement was growing in strength,
Thatcher appointed Heseltine as Minister of Defence.
One specific part of his job is to discredit CND;
such is the nature of Conservative democracy.

As pacifists we are too easily forced back into tokenism,
making hollow gestures against the wheels of the juggernaut.
The line is delicate.
The spaces have always been created by the gentle and caring,
to be later filled by bullies and egotists.
We can try to fill those spaces with the strength of our love.
Gandhi called it 'Ahimsa'.
The Greenham Woman call it the 'Politics of Whimsy',
but it doesn't end there, neither is it enough.

Gandhi played a major role in liberating India from British rule,
but conditions in India are still appaling for the ordinary people.
Limiting Greenham Peace Camp to women only
        is a sensible political ploy,
but if it is a demonstration of sexual exclusivity it is a sham.
Aren't we seeking to destroy all forms of exclusivity?
Does our own oppression give us the right to oppress others?
Unless we are prepared to oppose all oppression,
we stand guilty of direct contribution to it.

The neo-fascists plunder our land
and we must resist them on every level.
As outsiders we have few rights with which to oppose them,
but on our own, together, we seek them.
They have their law and those who impose it.
We only have ourselves and each other.
They have their order and those who impose it.
We only have ourselves and each other.
It is easy to dismiss those who seek peace as dreamers,
but isn't our whole culture built on past dreams?
It is essential that our dreams become a reality
or there will cease to be one.

Harrods boasts that it can supply any whim that its wealthy
        clients might express,
well let them supply me an Exocet missile and a
        starving Third World child
and I'll teach them the politics of choice.
Equality doesn't enter into the ghettos of wealth.
Beneath the protective sheath of Thatcher's economy
the right, rich and privileged get ever richer
and they, in turn, support her barbaric policies
        both at home and overseas.

1983

The Falklands War cost Britain over
        sixteen thousand million pounds—in whose pocket?
Throughout the world millions of people
        are employed making armaments,
Don't they realise that it's ordinary people like themselves
        who'll suffer the effects of their filthy labour?

The wealthy obscene with their obscene wealth
applaud the carnage from their grandstand.
It's as if they were at Ascot laying their bets;
five to one on the Four Horsemen.

They believe that money can buy them out of the responsibility
that they have for the world that they bleed dry.
They are the true pornographers,
the real stylists in human perversion.
Rich educated tarts sit dumbly by,
watching their fortunes rise and fall
in the neatly pressed pin-striped trousers of the City:
débutante whores in rich men's castles.

The ruling élite with their puppet figurehead
Queen Elizabeth the Second, Regina Virgina,
strut about on the millions of bodies
that they have sacrificed to gain their position.
Who are these leaders but those who have made violence pay?
Who are they but the inheritors of their ancestors greed and theft?
Their blood stained flags are rags to our future,
tattered remnants of our individual rights.

These rulers are common murderers and thieves,
but still we bow before them.
For how long will the masses
be so pathetically manipulated by God, Queen and Country?

For fuck's sake where are we in all this?
We're given life yet we court death.
For Christ's sake how long? How long, oh Lord, how long?
Still we lay prostrate before a stylised figure on a crucifix,
as if the stone fool might be resurrected.
We are expected to bargain our lives for his
and join him in the ugliness of perpetual Christian guilt.
He hangs there as a reminder of our own subjugation.
Let it be known that he alone is Christ,
those who dare emulate him shall suffer thus.
Each settlement is spiked with that stupid image,
each conscience nailed to that diet of corruption.

Military acts are bathed in those gory tales.
Tired marines, edgy to fuck and sleep, are blessed in his name.
Pious virgins in desire kneel in worship before the myth;
in anticipation of their own death, they await his coming.
Sweet Jesus, have mercy on me.
Sweet Jesus, they share his agony.
Sweet Jesus, they share his misery.
Fuck his loaded deity.

. . .

1983

Over half the world's population is starving,
crucified by the greed of landowners,
helpless against the imbalance of priorities
practised by the major powers who, if they wanted to, could help.
Every minute of the day millions upon millions of pounds
are spent on the machinery of war.
If only a half of that was spent on the machinery of peace,
there would be no more starvation on this planet.
Yet governments pay no heed to the cries of suffering,
they perhaps make token gestures to appease their consciences,
but no real improvements are made
because, to ensure control, the superpowers need to maintain
      the imbalance.
Natives are slaughtered in their homelands
by governments seeking out new possessions.
Most of the wealth of the so-called developed nations
has been gained at the expense of the Third World
from whom natural resources, both mineral and human,
have been unscrupulously exploited.
Peoples' pride and dignity is burnt in Napalm
and hand-held flame-throwers.
The poor and underprivileged are raped and tormented
by leaders who use their power not to assist, but to oppress.
At the wave of a gloved hand
these people can, and do,
send young men to their deaths,
but not before others too have fallen from their bayonets and guns.
Such armies are invariably called 'peace-keeping forces'.
The hypocrisy is as appalling as it is obvious.
The wealthy, educated, privileged and secure
make the lives of those less fortunate a complete misery.

Millions upon millions of people are dying from malnutrition
because, to stabilise their economies, governments destroy food
    rather than giving it to the needy.

"Let them eat cake" said Marie Antoinette
as she wiped the calf's blood from her lips.

"Proud to be British" said Margaret Thatcher
as she wiped the Falklands' blood from her hands.

The ruling élite have no concept of what it is to suffer want,
yet it is they who are directly responsible.
In a world where there are people who can't afford a crust of bread,
these arrogant scabs drive around in Bentleys and Rolls Royces.
Perhaps it amuses them to rub shit into the faces of the poor,
but there'll come a time when such overt displays of wealth
will not be tolerated by the people in the street.
In a sane society wealth and possession would not be an asset.

A few years ago, a politician was on the radio
saying that no one in the UK suffered from want.
Next day I saw an old man pleading for a handful of coal;
his wife was dying of cold and he was penniless.
Maybe in the morning, as the politician sipped breakfast tea,
she lay cold and dead before the empty grate.
Every year, thousands of people die of hypothermia,
too hungry, too cold, too poor to stay alive.

At times of national crisis it's always the poor who suffer.
'Back Britain', we're told
as the rich get richer and the poor get poorer.
At times of international crisis it's the same story.

'Back Britain,' we're told
as the rich get richer and the poor get killed.
In the event of a nuclear crisis,
the rich will retreat to private bunkers with their
        wealth and possessions.

The injustice of inequality is sanctioned by the church.
With its tradition of finance from the gentry,
the church has always been obliged
to ensure that its flock remains servile.

"Repent ye sinners or be devoured in the flames of hell."
Those very same flames that devoured their enemies
        in countless religious wars.

So often the church has marched hand in hand with the military,
casting its blessings upon the writhing bodies of the battlefield.
Each stab of bayonet is God's word.
Each crash of steel is God's word.
Each torn limb and splash of blood is God's word.
For he so loved the world he gave our only begotten sons.
Each sodden grave and sodding death is God's word.
For he so loved the world he gave our only begotten sons.

In Christian societies, executions
        are attended by representatives of the church.
Goggle-eyed before the gallows,
        the electric chair and the gas-chamber
they administer their Christ's blessing.
In America poison is injected into the bloodstream.
Another Christ dies, jacked up by the State.
Another glorious advance for civilisation.

One small step for man,
one giant step for mankind.
For he so loved the world
he gave us his only begotten son
and likewise we are expected so to do.
For he so loved the world.
Violent, vicious hypocrisy.
How is anyone supposed to deal with these contradictions,
confusions and lies? They defy reason.
Oh yes, you can inwardly laugh at the absurdity,
satirise the obscenity, but the hysteria soon wears thin
and the tears wear a colder complexion.
Humour can offer diversion,
but it dilutes real anger
and nothing gets confronted.
We are ruled by dangerous mad-people;
what's funny about that for fuck's sake?
The world is daily threatened with annihilation;
is that really something to be trivialised?
The world is under constant threat.
Against this background of fear
we struggle to create our own authority.
While being bludgeoned into conformity,
we struggle to find our inner-selves.
Of course I feel uncomfortable when I'm laughed at in the streets,
but I don't want to be one of them.
I want to be an outsider,
at the same time I'd like to come in out of the cold.

Urgency overrules personal fears.
Against the scenario of total destruction
we demand a sanity that might save the world.

1983

That alone excludes us from the mainstream of thought.
History offers no solutions,
quotes from Mao or Stalin, Hitler or Marx
simply confirm the oppression.
I'm tired of political experts,
tired of 'if onlys'.
They have always been the same people;
grey, visionless robots
who would have us all share their death.
History is simply a justification for oppression,
written by those who practise it.
It is being constantly changed and rewritten
to conform to the requirements of the ruling élite;
a tempest of convenience
that blasts across the blistered bodies of the dead.
We receive at best only filtered truths.
Most of what we see and hear is lies.

The Falklands War was rewritten as it happened.
It was not a glorious victory for the British spirit,
nor an heroic defeat of a fascist dictator.
It was a callous and savage piece of electioneering
designed to cover up horrific domestic problems.
At a time when a peaceful settlement was a possibility,
Thatcher personally ordered the sinking of the General Belgrano,
killing over three hundred men
and horribly mutilating many more.
She did this because her political neck required bloodshed
to prove her wisdom in releasing the Task Force.
The history books will not document her as
        a cold-blooded murderer.

1983

I'm tired of the dull rationalisation of the politicians,
weighed down with their sums and inadequacies
I feel only anger and bellied hatred for them.
How can anyone become so distorted?
How can anyone be so far from real human values?
I feel only disgust for their twisted minds.
How can peace be achieved through threats of violence?
What kind of hope is there in that straitjacket?

The authority of those who oppress us
is supported, maintained and defended
by those who are themselves the most oppressed;
those who, because they have no alternative,
        are in service to the rulers.

How can I feel anger towards the squaddy?
Weighed down with his guns and inadequacies
I can feel only pity and bellied compassion.
How can anyone be so distorted?
How can anyone be so far from real human values?
I can only feel pity for his twisted mind.
How can freedom be achieved if the poor fight to uphold
the privileges of those who directly oppress them?

We look through one eye hoping the other won't see,
that way we only need deal with a half of it.
Like bloody ostriches, oblivious,
not because we are, but because we choose to be.
Most people see through the lies,
but are too afraid to admit it.
It's so much easier to be the passive observer.
How much longer can people afford to just sit by like this?

All the indications are there:
massive unemployment,
recession, depression.
But who's looking? Who cares?
Tamely the population is being led down the road to total bondage.
Government is daily strengthening its powers.
Those who stand against it are ridiculed,
discredited or abused and punished.
Those in power are totally cynical.
Rather than analysing the seriousness of the problem,
they simply strengthen the army and police to combat it.
They are ready for the inevitable response.
It happened in Brixton, Toxteth and Moss Side.
It happens daily in Northern Ireland.
Under Thatcher's regime there have been massive increases
        in police brutality.
In London, police shot down a man
only to find it was the wrong person.
We regret to inform you, regret to inform you,
regret to inform you. We regret to inform you
that today another Christ was shot in the back of the head.
We regret to inform you, regret to inform you
that another Christ, not yet ten years old, was shot today
by agents of Her Majesty's Government, with a plastic bullet.
They say that plastic bullets are designed not to kill;
they do.
I say that human beings were not designed to kill, not us, not me;
we do.
We regret to inform you.

'Nineteen Eighty-Four' is a book about the positive danger of
        totalitarianism;
under Thatcher's unfeeling guidance the scenario is one year early.

With the cold mechanism of the pin-ball arcade
we're flicked around as numbers by the hidden computers:
software in the hardware, documented and filed.
We have no access to the information that they have stored on us.
Ticker-tape alter egos, print-out portraits,
we are becoming another.
As individuals within that mechanical system we are arbitrary,
wanted only for what can be taken from us.
Our future is of no concern to the mega-corporations
who determine the nature of our economic well-being.
Thatcher's policies require massive unemployment
which makes her order to 'support our boys'
        nothing but a fucking insult.
When they were eight thousand miles away dying for
        her arrogance,
she fabricated what was a complete mockery of compassion.
When they're at home, jobless on the streets,
she doesn't give a fuck for them.
Self-determination and self-enterprise are her big lines,
but just how much of that does she offer to others?
In her contemptible use of people
she was prepared to risk world peace,
saying that it was for the self-determination of the Falklanders,
those very same people who over a year ago
she was prepared to abandon without a thought.
And now, for all her empty talk,
they are forced to live in a fortress waiting for further hostilities.
Thatcher has recently sanctioned a loan of one hundred million
        pounds to Argentina,
claiming that it was to stabilise world economy.
The purchase of further Exocets
        and the development of nuclear potential

1983

should do much for world economy,
     but very little for world security.
Just what the fuck was all that bloodshed for?

Thatcher has signed away British self-determination in one
     single stroke.
She has agreed to install deadly Cruise Missiles on British soil
over which the Americans have total control.
The American military presence is designed solely
to limit nuclear war with Russia to the 'European Theatre'.
Meanwhile we are sold the wicked lie
     of protection and deterrence.
American war planners have repeatedly stated that they intend
to fight the Third World War on European soil;
Cruise Missiles greatly increase the danger of that happening.
Designed to avoid radar detection by
     skimming the earth's surface,
Cruise Missiles are seen as the ideal 'first strike weapon';
they also guarantee a massive response
     that would make Britain into a nuclear desert.
Military naïvety is astounding. The experts seriously believe
that they will be able to limit war to the 'theatre'.
In this particular show the world will be the stage.
There'll be no encore.

Thatcher and her cronies talk of 'limited tactical response'
and 'executive action' causing 'collateral damage'.
These terms are borrowed from their American counterparts
and are designed to mask the ugly reality that they describe.
In everyday language 'collateral damage' simply means
     civilian deaths.
In the event of nuclear attack on Britain,
     that would amount to thirty-eight million people.

Is it any wonder that these crazy psychotics
invent jargon to assist them in their studied madness?
Every year hundreds of innocent people still die horrific deaths
as a result of the bombs dropped on Hiroshima and Nagasaki.
It is probable that an all out nuclear war
would destroy all life on planet Earth.

We are not talking fantasy,
nor preaching doom.
We are talking of an existing reality;
the one that we allow to exist around us.

Defence Secretary Heseltine disputes
        the kind of information that we offer,
claiming that it has 'no basis in fact'.
There are no words to describe the utter contempt
that we feel for people of his kind.
They sit in their seats of power
distorting and perverting all human decency.
How can they dare be so blatant?
How can they dare be so hypocritical?
Who is this Heseltine with his corrupt lies?
Who is this Thatcher with her arrogant deceit?
These hideous mutants cast their shadows
across all that is worthwhile and good.

Cruise Missiles will be installed because Thatcher has created
        some kind of deal with Reagan.
We will probably never know the details of that arrangement.
It will almost certainly involve some kind
        of economic juggling act;
the massive corporations turning political thumbscrews
on US investment in Britain.

x

1983

[87]

Russian tanks in Afghanistan are nothing
compared with the bargaining power of
        American capital in the UK.
Whatever the nature of that deal is,
it has made Britain into America's front line;
the Fifty-Third State, with no rights of citizenship.
To many people that might not matter;
fed from birth on American propaganda and Hollywood trash,
the resistance levels are low.
As long as we passively accept American domination,
we can expect no real advance.
We are being sold down the line.

To many people the missiles and warheads might not matter.
To many people nuclear reality is too huge to contemplate,
yet for all people the reality looms constantly in nightmares.
In the nuclear State we are expected to accept those nightmares.
Is this really all that we can hope for as life?
Is this really all that we can hope for as death?
Maybe our lives don't matter that much,
but why impose our madness on future generations?
Or is it perhaps that you no longer believe
        that there will be future generations?
In your passive acceptance of it,
you have already allowed the holocaust to happen.
The future is ended.

We are not talking fantasy,
nor preaching doom.
We are talking of an existing reality,
the one that we allow to exist around us.

The nuclear hardware produced in the last three decades
will pollute the Earth for thousands of years.
A nuclear war will destroy it.
Is that why the cherry trees blossom?
You are destroying and corrupting.
In condemning them to the nuclear nightmare,
are you willing to accept the burning of tomorrow's unborn?
They know nothing of this sorrow.

Suffer little children to come unto me.
Suffer little children to come unto me.
Suffer little children to come unto me.
Suffer little children to come unto me.

In your refusal to act against these hideous dangers
you are guilty of being the gutless passive observer.
Are you so inhuman that you will let this happen,
just a helpless bystander waving your flag in mute acceptance?
Take up your eyes and see.
Take up your ears and hear.
Take up your mind and think.
Take up your life and act.

It is up to us all as responsible citizens of Earth
to work towards the downfall of the powerful élite.
Their rule has created dreadful suffering.
Their insanity precludes all reason and compassion.
They lie, trick and manipulate.
They are the maggots in the flesh of decency,
the vultures that pick at the bones of hope,
the carriers of famine, war, pestilence, and death.

They must be stopped.
Why should people die for their insanity?
Why should people starve for their insanity?
Why should people suffer the spitefulness of their greed?
We must not be intimidated by the authority
that they appear to have.
We must be prepared to oppose them on every level,
to fight back in the knowledge that if we don't
we will have failed in our responsibility to life itself.
It has happened before
that the powerless have risen against the oppressor
only to be beaten back.
But there have been cases
where they have succeeded.
Ours is a just cause;
it is up to each one of us, alone, to do our best.
We must learn to overcome our fears.
We must realise that the strength that they have
is the strength that we give them.
It is you, the passive observer, who has given them this power.
You are being used and abused
and will be discarded as soon as they've bled
        what they want from you.

You must learn to live with your own conscience,
                    your own morality,
                    your own decision,
                    your own self.

You alone can do it.

There is no authority but yourself.

One squaddy, horrifically burnt in the Falklands War, was approached by Prince Charles during a presentation. "Get well soon" said the Prince, to which the squaddy replied, "Yes, Sir, I will".

HOW DOES IT FEEL
(TO BE THE MOTHER OF A THOUSAND DEAD)?

PENNY RIMBAUD

WHEN YOU WOKE THIS MORNING YOU LOOKED SO ROCKY-EYED,
blue and white normally, but strange ringed like that in black.
It doesn't get much better,
your voice can get just ripped up shouting in vain.
Maybe someone hears what you say,
but you're still on your own at night.

You've got to make such a noise to understand the silence,
screaming like a jackass,
ringing ears so you can't hear the silence, even when it's there,
like the wind seen from the window;
seeing it,
but not being touched by it.

We never asked for war,
nor in the innocence of our birth
were we aware of it.
We never asked for war,
nor in the struggle to realisation
did we feel there was a need for it.
We never asked for war,
nor in the joyful colours of our childhood
were we conscious of its darkness.

HOW DOES IT FEEL?

1982

How does it feel to be the mother of a thousand dead?
Young boys rest now, cold graves in cold earth.
How does it feel to be the mother of a thousand dead?

Sunken eyes, lost now: empty sockets in futile death.
Your arrogance has gutted these bodies of life,
your deceit fooled them that it was worth the sacrifice.
Your lies persuaded people to accept the wasted blood,
your filthy pride cleansed you of the doubt you should have had.
You smile in the face of death because you are so proud and vain,
your cruel inhumanity stops you from realising the pain
that you inflicted,
you determined, you created, you ordered—
it was your decision to have those young boys slaughtered.

You never wanted peace or solution,
from the start you lusted after war and destruction.
Your blood-soaked reason ruled out other choices,
your mockery gagged more moderated voices.
So keen to play your bloody part,
so impatient that your war be fought,
Iron Lady with your stone heart
so eager that the lesson be taught,
that you inflicted,
you determined, you created, you ordered—
it was your decision to have those young boys slaughtered.

Throughout our history you and your kind have stolen the young
bodies of the living to be twisted and torn in filthy war.
What right have you to defile those births?
What right have you to devour that flesh?

1982

What right to spit on hope
with the gory madness that you inflicted,
you determined, you created, you ordered?
It was your decision to have those young boys slaughtered.

How does it feel to be the mother of a thousand dead?
Young boys rest now, cold graves in cold earth.
How does it feel to be the mother of a thousand dead?

You accuse us of disrespect for the dead,
but it was you who slaughtered out of national pride.
Just how much did you care?
What respect did you have
as you sent those bodies to their communal grave?
You buried them rough-handed, they'd given you their all,
that once-living flesh defiled in the hell that you inflicted,
you determined, you created, you ordered —
it was your decision to have those young boys slaughtered.

You use those deaths to achieve your ends still,
using the corpses as a moral blackmail.
You say "Think of what those young men gave"
as you try to bind us in your living death,
yet we do think of them,
ice-cold and silenced in the snow-covered moorlands,
stopped by the violence that you inflicted,
you determined, you created, you ordered —
it was your decision to have those young boys slaughtered.

1982

THE IMMORTAL DEATH

GEE VAUCHER

OUR BOYS HAVE RETURNED AS MEN, OUR MEN.
Our men have returned, amen.

The spoils of war, the hero, the lads,
    men pulled together for war,
        set out to fight for the great British flag
           that was waved by the thousands ashore.
Waving farewell,
    the girls bare it all and pull up their jumpers and skirts,
        carried away the crowd calls for more and the men felt
        it worth fighting for.
It's all gone before, sexy Sue, saucy Jane,
    the pin-up that's carried to battle,
        the mascot that marks in every plane,
          every gun, markers of death,
            symbols of men in whose name we are
             slaughtered like cattle.

In every good war there's a nude on the wall
    to keep the men happy and straight.
A saucy old joke, lads, it's all harmless fun,
    when we hit land who shall we rape?
Ah, the spoils of war, the knickers, the bras;
    momentos to give you support.
While the bombs drop around,
    you fumble in dreams with blank eyes,
        see the corpses you've fought.

Our boys have gone away, our boys,
our boys have gone away.
Our men have returned all tattered and burned,
our men have returned, amen.

The guns point their muzzles away to the land and
        below deck the men throw darts.
The nipples are bulls-eyes, the head counts for less,
        and there's no points for hitting the heart.
Shapely Jane, twenty-five, said "Those lovely real he-men
        no red-blooded girl can deny are there for the taking,
                but it's all so frustrating if you're married
                        and already tied."
But bare it all girls and have all the dreams
        of dashing young soldiers so brave.
Send him a garter, a cross, love ever after,
        for soon he will be in his grave.
Ah, those rotting young men who all did their duty
        are sinking away in the sea,
                and they've missed, just for them,
                        the 'Invincible panties', displayed in the *Sun*,
                                page three.

The bodies of war, the pin-up, the corpse,
        flesh that is perfect and torn;
the breast that is curved, that is pink and seductive,
        the breast that is ripped and laid bare;
the beckoning arms, the legs that are parted,
        the welcoming look and the wink;
the arms that are shredded, the legs that are no more,
        the face that is rotten and stinks.
The sickness of war, the men gone before,
        good luck and God speed you away.

1982

The madonna is there,
            stripped naked and bare on the door.
                    She will show you the way.

Our boys have gone away, our boys,
our boys have gone away.
Our men have returned all tattered and burned,
our men have returned, amen.

User, abuser,
            the conquering man,
                        makes use of the spoils of war.
Confirming the glory,
            the woman is raped and the soldiers re-name her as 'whore'.
Their bodies are torn and disfigured,
            in their heads life is never the same.
From the wall saucy Sal is still smiling
            as the nightmare is caught in his pain.
Her body still perfect and tempting
            is blistered with blood of his tears.
His body confused and still frightened
            turns from the truth that he fears;
his friends that were killed for the reason
            of war that is fought over lies.
The pin-up remains ever after,
            immortal as all around dies.

Our boys have returned as men, our men,
our men have returned again.
Our men have returned all tattered and burned,
our men have returned, amen.

1982

DON'T TELL ME YOU CARE

JOY DE VIVRE

YOU SHIT-HEAD SLIMY GOT IT ALLS.
You crap-eyed ghosts with greasy balls.
You wicked matron stabbing hard,
    grabbing while the going's good.
Administrators' vicious smile
    dancing on the body-pile,
        slipping your sly fingernails,
            impaling flesh on battlefields.
The decaying corpses help you up
    to your position at the top.

You shit-head slimy want it alls.
You bind the baby as it crawls
    and crush its head, the soft new skull,
        burst its brain and keep it dull.
You own its mind, you murderous thief,
    grind it down with bloodied teeth
        and feed it up with national pride . . .
progress through self-sacrifice,
    not for themselves, but you, you scab,
        you raid the bodies of the dead.

You shit-head slimy make it alls
    with dead meat dripping as you walk;
        don't talk of justice or respect
            you shit-soaked armchair moralist . . .

what right is yours that others' lives
                are yours to smash and kill and bind?
It's your security that they bleed for,
        your definitions that they die for ...
                you stack your dead heroes
                        with no more thought
                                than some accountant at their work.

You shit-head slimy got it alls,
        crap-eyed ghosts where maggots crawl,
                tired old jerk-offs with your bodyguards;
        those muscle-pimps with forty-fives,
                you gutless automatic butchers,
                        bullet shitting dumbhead hookers,
                                it's your heartless failure they protect
                                        while you deny the shame of your neglect.
All you can see is your brutal success
        and damn the dead and fear the mess.

You shit-head greedy have it alls,
        you cheat and lie and jargonise
                that your success is also ours,
                        that which you take you take for us
                                while your ambition scrapes the living dry
                                        and your solutions are archaic battlecries.
You dead meat eyesore death pushers,
        look elsewhere for your arse-lickers ...
The face that stares back from the mirror
        reflects the reality of your horror.

1982

So don't tell me you care, shithead.
You betray the dead as you curse life.
Eat your own shit, leader of the nation,
        piss off to your Downing Street fortress,
leave us out of your madness,
        buy your own Vaseline,
                grease your own arse,
                        shit in your own back-yard,
                        suck your own turds ...
                        THIS IS OUR WORLD.

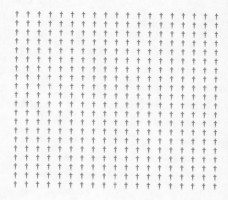

1982

SHEEP FARMING IN
THE FALKLANDS

PENNY RIMBAUD

We are interrupting this programme to make a special announcement. At four o'clock this morning, British Standard Time, Britain's Premier, Margaret Thatcher, called an emergency summit meeting with the Foreign Secretary, Lord Carrington, in the board room of Ten Downing Street. A five o'clock deadline had been set to find a solution to the increasingly tense situation in the Fulklands. Mrs Thatcher is said to have been moist with anticipation as Lord Carrington entered the door nervously holding the knob. The eyes of the nation were on Mrs Thatcher as she confidently slipped her hand into her brief. She knew that the little red button now at her fingertips could unleash an orgy of physical combat. As she commanded Lord Carrington to make an entry, she knew that she would soon feel the weight of power upon her shoulders. She had always covered up in the past, but the imminent possibility of close combat obliged her to reveal all. After running through the usual preliminaries, Lord Carrington felt abreast of the situation and Mrs Thatcher was delighted to show him the little red button and demonstrate its uses, most notably its connection to the hot-line receiver. To enable him to get on top of the job, Lord Carrington was ordered to get seriously stuck in and at all costs, because of the gravity of the situation, to avoid simply running through the motions. Nervously he touched the little red button, but as Mrs Thatcher excitedly pushed it towards him, his fingers slipped and he missed the mark, leaving the Premier feeling well browned off. However, not to be frustrated by the weakness of others, Mrs Thatcher determined to finish the job herself and, having dismissed the unfortunate Lord Carrington, grabbed the hotline telephone and put the receiver to it's devilish work. Within seconds the hotline was a frenzy of activity and after years of anticipation Mrs Thatcher's forces were heading towards a climax, sliding apprehensively towards endless oceans: an unstoppable power breaking through the briny. This was her finest moment and, at its peak, she cried, "England expects every man to do his best. I know nothing of failure. We are going to win."

SHEEP FARMING IN THE FALKLANDS,
re-arming in the fucklands,
fucking sheep in the homelands,
Her Majesty's forces are coming...

1983

Fuck off to the Falklands for your sea-faring fun,
big man's jerk off dreamland, looking down the barrel of a gun.
Friggin in the riggin, another imperialist farce,
another page of British history to wipe the national arse.
The royals donated Prince Andrew as a show of their support,
was it just luck the only ship that wasn't struck,
was the one on which he fought?
Three cheers for good old Andy, let's take a pic for his mum,
And stick it up the royal, stick it up the royal,
Stick it up the royal album...

Sheep farming in the Falklands,
re-arming in the fucklands,
fucking sheep in the homelands,
Her Majesty's forces are coming...

Onward Thatcher's soldiers, it's your job to fight ...

> *"And, you know, I don't really give a toss. If the cause is*
> *wrong or right. My political neck means more to me than the*
> *lives of a thousand men. If I felt it might be of use to me, I'd*
> *do it all over again. The Falklands was really a cover-up job,*
> *it obscured the mistakes I've made, and, you know I think the*
> *gamble I took could certainly be said to have paid. With*
> *unemployment at an all-time high and the country falling*
> *apart, I, Winston Thatcher, reign supreme in this great*
> *nation's heart"* ...

Sheep farming in the Falklands,
re-arming in the fucklands
fucking sheep in the homelands,
Her Majesty's forces are coming ...

While the men who fought her battles are still expected to suffer,
Thatcher proves in Parliament that she's just a fucking nutter ...

The Iron Lady's proved her metal, has struck with her fist of steel,
has proved that a heart that is made out of lead is

a heart that doesn't feel.

Now Thatcher says ...

> *"Oh raunchy Ron, we've fought our war, now it's your turn*
> *to prove yourself in El Salvador. I've employed Michael*
> *Heseltine to deal with PR. He's an absolute prick, but a*
> *media star. He'll advocate the wisdom of our Cruise Missile*
> *plan, then at last I'll have a penis just like every other man.*
> *They can call it penis envy, but they'll pay the price for it ..."*
> *"But the peasants are hungry, Mags."*
> *"Let them eat shit ..."*

Sheep farming in the Falklands,
re-arming in the fucklands,
fucking sheep in the homelands,
Her Majesty's forces are coming ...

Who the fuck cares, we're all having fun?
Mums and dads happy as their kids play with guns,
the media loved it, when all's said and done.
'Britain's bulldog's off the leash' said the *Sun,*
as the Argies and Brits got crippled or died,
the bulldog turned around and crapped in our eyes.
Brit-wit, hypocrite, don't you yet realise
you're not playing with toys, you're playing with lives?
You piss straight up in your self-righteous rage;
wilfs, goms and gimps in the nuclear age.
Four minute warning, what a shock, well balls to you, rocket cock,
you're old and you're ill and you're soon going to die,
you've got nothing to lose as you fill up the skies.
You'd take us all with you, yeah, it's tough at the top,
you slop bucket, shit filled, puss ridden, death pimp snot ...
YAH FUCK.

GOTCHA!

PENNY RIMBAUD

GOTCHA, YOU ARGIE BASTARD, YOU FUCKING SPIK,
 you latin bender, you dago prick ...
Gotcha, gotcha, gotcha, gotcha, gotcha, gotcha, gotcha, gotcha.
Our boys have got it right ...

Right now, rule Britannia, Britain rules the waves,
Britain never, never, never will be slaves.
Gotcha, you Argie bastard, you dago gimp,
 you motherfucker, you greasy pimp ...

Gotcha, gotcha, gotcha, gotcha, gotcha, gotcha, gotcha, gotcha.
Our boys have got it right ...

Right now, God save Her Majesty, raise the Union Jack.
God save Margaret Thatcher, she'll claim our empire back ...

Right now, right now, right now, right now, right now, right now,
right now, right now, right now, Thatcher's got it right ...

This is Thatcher's Britain, built on national pride,
built on national heritage and the bodies of those who died
 to wave the flag on the Falklands,
to protect us from the Irish hordes, to support the rich
 in their difficult task of protecting themselves from the poor.
Yes, this is Thatcher's Britain,
so let's increase the strength of the police,
let's expand the military, let's all arm for peace,

let's suppress all opposition, let's keep the people down,
let's resurrect past histories for the glory of the crown ...

Right now, right now, right now, right now, right now, right now,
right now, right now, right now, Thatcher's got it right ...

Right now, God save Prince Charlie,
God bless his wife,
God bless their fortune,
God bless their privileged life ...

Gotcha, gotcha, gotcha, gotcha, gotcha, gotcha, gotcha, gotcha.
Our men have got it right ...

Gotcha, you Argie bastard, you fucking arsehole, you bloody wog.
Right now, let's back Britain, let's tighten up it's laws,
let's up and atom, let's rally to the cause ...

Gotcha, gotcha, gotcha, gotcha, gotcha, gotcha, gotcha, gotcha.
Thatcher's got it right ...

Gotcha, you Argie bastards, you Commie scum,
        you bloody scoundrel, you Paki bum,
you thieving Arab, you slit-eyed gook,
        you dirty browner, you pacifist poof,
you senile cripple, you dirty whore,
        we'll get all the benders and many more.

1983

WHO DUNNIT?

TONES & JEREMY RATTER PLUS ALL AND SUNDRY

BIRDS PUT THE TURD IN CUSTARD,
    but who put the shit in Number Ten?
Birds put the turd in custard, but who put the shit in Number Ten?
Birds put the turd in custard, but who put the shit in Number Ten?
Well strike a bleedin' light, did I get the message right?
    They say the shit's back in Number Ten again ...

Birds put the turd in custard, but who put the shit in Number Ten?
Birds put the turd in custard, but who put the shit in Number Ten?
Birds put the turd in custard, but who put the shit in Number Ten?
Well what a fucking joke, it's enough to make you choke
    'cos the shit's back in Number Ten again ...

Birds put the turd in custard, but who put the shit in Number Ten?
Birds put the turd in custard, but who put the shit in Number Ten?
Birds put the turd in custard, but who put the shit in Number Ten?
Well I can't believe my ears, after four horrific years
    the shit's back in Number Ten again ...

Birds put the turd in custard, but who put the shit in Number Ten?
Birds put the turd in custard, but who put the shit in Number Ten?
Birds put the turd in custard, but who put the shit in Number Ten?
Was it just a force of habit? In and out just like a rabbit,
    the shit's back in Number Ten again ...

1983

We know who put the turd in Britain,
     but who put the shit in Number Ten?
We know who put the boot in Brixton,
     but who put the shit in Number Ten?
We know who put the Brits in Belfast,
     but who put the shit in Number Ten?
You'd think it was enough, but then she called the Falklands' bluff
     and the shit's back in Number Ten again ...

. . .

Birds put the turd in custard, but who put the shit in Number Ten?
Birds put the turd in custard, but who put the shit in Number Ten?
Birds put the turd in custard, but who put the shit in Number Ten?
Well, I ask you, dense or what? We're gonna cop the fucking lot
     'cos the shit's back in Number Ten again ...

We know who pulled the chain on Britain,
     but who put the shit in Number Ten?
We know who's gonna make the people pay for it,
     but who put the shit in Number Ten?
We know who waves the flag for Queen & Country,
     but who put the shit in Number Ten?
You might just fucking smile, but in true blue Tory style,
     the shit's back in Number Ten again ...

      — I say, I say, I say; what's the difference between a
       cactus and the Houses of Parliament?
      — I don't know. What is the difference between a
       cactus and the Houses of Parliament?
      — A cactus has got its pricks on the outside.

Birds put the turd in custard, but who put the shit in Number Ten?
Birds put the turd in custard, but who put the shit in Number Ten?
Birds put the turd in custard, but who put the shit in Number Ten?

> — *I say, I say, I say; what's the difference between a pair*
> *of Margaret Thatcher's knickers and the Union Jack?*
> — *I don't know. What is the difference between a pair of*
> *Margaret Thatcher's knickers and the Union Jack?*
> — *The Union Jack hasn't got any brown stripes on it.*

We know who put the johnny on Ark Royal,
  but who put the shit in Number Ten?
And when the bugger comes, we'll have have a nice cruise,
  but who put the shit in Number Ten?
Thatcher's smiling out her arse but it ain't funny,
  but who put the shit in Number Ten?
And if the bombers come at last, stick a finger up your arse
  'cos the shit's back in Number Ten …

Birds put the turd in custard, but who put the shit in Number Ten?
Birds put the turd in custard, but who put the shit in Number Ten?
Birds put the turd in custard, but who put the shit in Number Ten?
It's enough to make you laugh 'cos it's another Tory farce
  'cos the shit's back in Number Ten again …

1983

NAGASAKI IS YESTERDAY'S DOG-END

GEE VAUCHER

ATTENTION. FUCK AMERICAN POWER.
Fuck Russian power. Fuck British power.

ATTENTION. These ignorant shits arm themselves for
annihilation and call it WORLD PEACE. Bollocks.

ATTENTION. Piss to the parties, the politicians,
the prat stud-men and their slaughter games.

ATTENTION. Reagan. Thatcher. Andropov. You stink and kill
this earth for your powerful silk-purse immorality.

ATTENTION. These rulers are already dead, murdered by their
own greed, and the world pays homage. Shit.

ATTENTION. It's fucking stupid to let so few run our lives
into death. Don't let them do it.

ATTENTION. Why the fuck do we allow this world to slowly die
from self-inflicted wounds? Tell me.

ATTENTION. Cruise missiles are at your door,
safely delivered for Christmas. Hooray.

ATTENTION. Big shit Heseltine assures us he will shoot anyone to
protect them. Who's fucking mad then?

1984

ATTENTION. In every country on the streets the police and army
protect the stage that's set for the holocaust.

ATTENTION. Trapped in their camp of concentrated filth they
expect us not to cut our way out. Scum.

ATTENTION. We refuse to take a bit-part in their pathetic
Hollywood nightmare, our reality.

ATTENTION. Stand up and fight.
Choose life or destruction, love or hate.
You cannot have both and survive.
Go forward.

Get out on the streets,
down the sewers.
Snap the rules,
creep through the net.

Fuck their diseased system.
The words are no longer enough.
The information has been given,
the lies have been exposed.

Choose your path.
It's time to fucking act.
No time to be nice.
It's time to fucking act.

1984

HAVE A NICE DAY

PENNY RIMBAUD

*Crass by name, even worse by nature, like it or not, they
just won't go away. Crass are the distempered dog end of rock
'n' roll's once bright and vibrant rebellion. That they're so
unattractive, unoriginal and badly unbalanced in an uncom-
promising and humourless sort of way, simply adds to the
diseased attraction of their naïvely black and white world
where words are a series of shock slogans and mindless token
tantrums to tout around your tribe and toss at passers by.*

*Good old Crass, our make believe secret society, our
let's pretend passport to perversity. They're nothing but a
caricature and a joke.*

— Tony Parsons

1982

SAME OLD STUFF, YOU'VE HEARD IT ALL BEFORE,
Crass being crass about the system, or is it war?
We ain't got no humour, we don't know how to laugh,
well if you don't fucking like it — fucking tough!

'Cos I'm the same old monkey in the same old zoo,
with the same old message trying to get through.
Screaming from the platform when the train ain't even there,
I've got a one way ticket, but I don't fucking care.

If what I've got to say is always much the same,
it's 'cos the game the system plays is still the same old game.
Senile idiots in their seats of power,
ancient rotting corpses breathing horror by the hour.

They're lovers of death those fucking creeps,
screwing our earth as our earth weeps.
Iron ladies and steel men,
waiting for their fucking war to start again.

Blood-lusting nutters plan death for us all,
they'll be hiding in their bunkers as we watch the missiles fall.
Ain't they just so decent, respectable and nice,
eating the fat of the land while it's us that pay the price?

Westminster's full of psychopaths with blood clots 'stead of brains,
flesh hungry vultures picking our remains,
shitting on the world they've shat on many times before,
fucked it good and proper, in the name of law.

Well bollocks to the lot of you, and you can fuck off too,
if you're bored with what I say, no one's asking you.

Just fuck off and have your fun,
hoist your Jolly Roger and wave your plastic gun,
with your painted faces and your elegant style,
how about trying to think for a while?

As you decorate your lifestyle with cheap consumer bliss,
forget about loving, it's your arse you're going to kiss.

As long as they've got you under their thumb
with TV lobotomy and media fun,
they'll have their way with you, what more can I say?
Watch out for the mind police, and have a nice day.

1982

NINETEEN EIGHTY BORE

PENNY RIMBAUD

WHO NEEDS A LOBOTOMY WHEN WE'VE GOT THE ITV?
Who needs ECT when there's good old BBC?
Switch on the set, light up the screen,
fantasise and dream about what you might have been.
Who needs controlling when they've got the cathode ray?
They've got your fucking soul, now they'll fuse your brains away.
Mindless fucking morons sit before the set
being fed the mindless rubbish they deserve to get.

Can't switch off Big Brother, they've lost all will to act.
Lost in drab confusion. Was it fiction? Was it fact?
Another plastic bullet stuns another Irish child,
but no one's really bothered, no, the telly keeps them mild.
They've lost all sense of feeling to the ever hungry glow,
drained of any substance by the vicious telly blow.
No longer know what's real or ain't, slowly going blind,
they stare into the goggle-box while the world goes by, behind.

The *Angels* are on TV tonight, grey puke, fucking shit.
The army occupy Ireland, but the boot will never fit.
Was it *Coronation Street*? Or was it Londonderry?
Oh it doesn't fucking matter, Paul Daniels'll keep us merry.
Yes, I've heard of Bobby Sands, wasn't it *Emmerdale Farm*?
Yes, that's right, he was kicked by a cow,
        I hope it didn't do him no harm.
And wasn't the Holocaust terrible, a good thing it wasn't for real.
Of course I've heard of H-Block, it's the baccy with man appeal.

Deeper and deeper and deeper, layer upon layer,
illusion, confusion, is there anyone left who can care?
Yes, the Abbey National cares for you, Nat West and Securicor.
Well bring out the Branston bren-guns, let's spice it up some more.
The Sweeney are cruising Brixton, they've created another Belfast,
and J.R.'s advising Thatcher on lighting, make up and cast.
A thousand camera lenses point at the people's pain,
as millions of mindless morons watch the action replay again.

                                action replay again.
                                action replay again.
                                action replay again.
                                action replay again.
                                action replay again.
                                action replay again.
                                action replay again.
                                action replay again.
                                action replay again.

Softly, softly, into your life, you're held in its brilliant glow.
Softly, softly, feeding itself on the you you'll never know.
Your life's reduced to nothing but an empty media game.
Big Brother ain't watching you, mate, you're fucking watching him.

1982

WHAT THE FUCK?

PENNY RIMBAUD

WHAT NOW? NOW YOU WOULD DESTROY THE EARTH,
dry, the river beds.
What now? Now in your control, birth and death,
dry, the bodies, incandescent in the heat.

Your fire is melting both soil and soul,
in plan maybe, is that not enough?
Your war and raving of it is so total,
you're consumed by it as you'd consume us.
Would you see the fire from your sanctuary of death?
What terrible pain you need to hide,
in your hatred you'd seek to destroy the earth;
what is it that you have been denied?
Your mind and its ranting are so barren;
what the fuck are you thinking? What the fuck?
Your eyes and their vision, empty, staring;
what the fuck are you seeing? What the fuck?

So singular your motives, yet impossible to define,
how finely lined my destiny in the cobwebs of your crime.
So insular your future, so alien your plan,
take all of this if you will and I'll take what I can.

A town that is no more,
"My God," you say, "what have I done?"
But you won't heed what's gone before,
"What pity?" you say, "There is none."

1981

[117]

And so you drive the world to war,
but this war will not be lost or won,
The desolation that you've seen but never saw,
is the lesson that you teach, but never learn.
But would you see the fire in the world where you exist?
Will your hard eyes register the pain?
Are you so cold that there is no distress?
Where there's death would you give death again?
No flowers in your landscape, some withered rose,
kicked amongst the corpses where they lay,
halted where all hope died, frozen,
by the horror of your acts compelled to stay.

Unnoticed all this in your lusting after death,
how determined that your darkness should be shared.
Unnoticed in your blindness this miracle of breath,
what element of beauty attracts your cruel desire?
Would you see the burning? Is that your delight?
Would you have me see it in your stead?
Would you feel my yearning? Peace, life, light,
body, breath. Would you take it all this?

What is it that you're seeking, so cold and so deprived?
What is it that you dream of in your empty eyeless head?
Why must I share your lust of death?
Can you not die alone?
Why must I share your fear of breath, light, life, PEACE?

1981

WOMEN

JOY DE VIVRE

FUCK IS WOMEN'S MONEY,
we pay with our bodies.
There's no purity in our love,
no beauty,
just bribery.
It's all the fucking same;
we make soldiers with our submission,
wars with our isolation.

Fuck is womens money,
we pay with our bodies.
There's no purity in motherhood,
no beauty,
just bribery.
It's all the fucking same;
we are all slaves to sexual histories.
Our awareness of whoredom can be a release.

War is men's money,
they pay with their bodies.
There is no purity in that game,
only blood, death and bribery.
It's still the fucking same,
but we have all got the power.
Don't just stand there and take submission on the strength of fear,
FIGHT WAR, NOT WARS

1978

BEG YOUR PARDON

PENNY RIMBAUD

BEG THE QUESTION, BEND THE TRUTH,
bail out the basement while there's holes in the roof.

In the beginning they said there was light,
well there ain't much left of it now.
We're lost in the darkness, searching sound and sight
of an answer to the what, where or how.
We're talking 'bout freedom while we're locked in a cell,
dreaming of a world without war,
forced to live on the boundaries of hell,
like no one's ever thought of peace before.
But what's the point of preaching peace
    if it's something you don't feel?
What's the point of talking love
    if you think that love ain't real?
Where's the hope in hopelessness?
Where's the truth in lies?
Don't hold my hand if you can't look me in the eyes.

Beg the question, bend the truth,
bail out the basement while there's holes in the roof.

In the beginning they said there was light,
but somebody's burnt out the fuse,
and now we're all lost in eternal night,
looking for a candle to use.

1982

Lots of little candles, isolated hope,
frail little flames in the gale,
lots of little people who just can't cope,
just knocking their heads on the nail.
What's the point of talking freedom
        if you just protect yourself?
What's the point of preaching sharing
        as you accumulate your wealth?
It's so easy to be giving if the things you give ain't real.
It's so easy to lie if you ignore the things you feel.

Beg the question, bend the truth,
bail out the basement while there's holes in the roof.

In the beginning they said there was light,
but we never had the eyes to see,
but rather than struggling or putting up a fight,
we ran like lemmings to the sea.
No one really wants to get it all together,
it's easier just to grab what you can.
Everybody's going it, hell for leather,
building little castles in the sand.
Hypocrisy, delusion, lies, pretence, deceit,
think only of yourself and the world's at your feet.
I don't believe the things you say, you make bullshit of the truth,
the game you play's offensive, and your life's the living proof.

Beg the question, bend the truth,
bail out the basement while there's holes in the roof.

1982

In the beginning they said there was light,
but I'm tired of hearing their lies.
I'm tired of deceit, gonna put up a fight,
I'm going to use my own eyes,
gonna make MY decisions, live my own life.
They can keep their darkness and gloom.
Hypocrisy, trickery, I've had enough.
They can keep their destruction and doom.
I've only one life and I'll live it my way,
they can keep their restrictions and law,
and it they think different I'll have one thing to say...
"Fuck off 'cos I've heard it before."

REALITY WHITEWASH

PENNY RIMBAUD

THE GREY MAN AT THE WHEEL
looks around to see if there's some skirt he can steal.
He doesn't really want to, he's just acting out a game,
and in their own fucked up way, most people do the same.
She cleans the bathroom mirror, so she can line her eyes,
an expert in delusion, an artist in disguise.
She's not content with what she is, but she does the best she can,
but she doesn't do it for herself, she does it for her man.

And meanwhile he's out hunting, this master of the hunt,
cruising down the high street in his endless search for cunt,
and the posters on the hoardings encourage his pursuit,
glossy ads where men are men, and women simply cute.
And the men are in their motorcars,
        and the men have nerves of steel,
and they dream of *Charlies Angels* as they firmly grip the wheel,
and they fantasise they're screwing in the back seat of the car,
fantasise they're fucking with a real-life movie star.
Fantasies to fill the gaps, to fill in every crack,
a whitewash on reality to hide the truth they lack.
Now she's sponging down the cooker, on the surface all is fine;
his dinner's in the oven 'cos he's doing overtime.
She switches on the telly, it makes her feel secure,
helps confirm her way of life, who needs to ask for more?
She sees the happy family, wife and hubby on the screen,
the perfect social unit, just like it's always been.

She's done the very best she can
to love and honour and obey her man,
and if she should ever doubt the wisdom of her choice,
she can turn to television for its moderating voice.
The ads and weekly series are the proof she needs
that a life of boredom outweighs the deeds.
She sits up 'til the epilogue and goes to bed alone,
content that when he's finished work he'll go straight home.

Meanwhile he downs another scotch, the lady has a coke,
and if he's asked about the wife he treats it as a joke.
"Hear the one about the you-know-what?"
He's got what it takes and he takes what he's got.
He took his woman and he'll take plenty more.
She took on a rat to keep the wolf from the door.
Then maybe in her loneliness she'll want to have a child
who'll be taught the games of adulthood: boxed and filed.

Another life to whitewash, to us a child is born
to follow in its parents' tracks, the path's well worn:
fantasy and falsehood, truth and lie,
the fucked up system they call reality.
The system needs its servants, each birth is one more.
They'll gently talk of freedom as they quietly lock the door
'cos the system needs its servants if the system's going to run,
needs its fodder for the workhouse, its targets for the gun.

1982

BIRTH CONTROL 'N' ROCK 'N' ROLL

JOY DE VIVRE

INDUSTRY ON THE MERCENARY BLOODPATH,
military loves the gory warbath,
economics shape the battle landscape,
all join together for the grand rape.

Moral intentions make a scapegoat,
excuse the rotting corpse inside the trenchcoat.

Praise the rotting minds above the club tie,
that sits in towers up in the blue sky,
above the clouds, obscure the scarred earth,
discuss manoeuvres, moves for more death,
arms make profit from the crushed head,
build the towers up on the ditch head.

Betrayal forms the formal skyline,
tinted windows catch the sunshine,
such ice cold beauty makes the heart sink,
five thousand miles away the dead stink.

And here the graveyard to insult them,
the city shines with laughing tombstones.

The profiteers, the warcry butchers,
stir up the lust for legal slaughter.

1982

The living dead who look up to them,
who accept authority that kills them,
work for the corporation making napalm.
Workers watch the burning children on TV
as they eat their meat pie with refusal in their mind's eye
to see their own lives in that cold death,
their state of wealth upon that lost breath.

In the official offices of deathplan,
leaders of men work to betray man.

Stocks and shares declare the next war,
the torture starts behind the locked door,
propaganda tops the big desk.

Compose an overture to fine death.

The hideous grey men of our nightmares dim the colour,
foul the clean air, their eyes forsake all that they dwell on,
drag the lover from the loved ones.

Patriot's progress is a backstep,
a cruel noose around a young neck.

They teach our children in the classroom
        to respect a madman on a rostrum,
to praise the dirty works of battle,
bring out the ribbon, balloon and rattle,
to dig their own graves in the cold earth ...
        so sad and pointless now to give birth.

1982

PUNK IS DEAD

PENNY RIMBAUD

YES THAT'S RIGHT, PUNK IS DEAD,
    it's just another cheap product for the consumers' head,
bubblegum rock on plastic transistors,
    schoolboy sedition backed by big-time promoters.
CBS promote The Clash,
    but it ain't for revolution, it's just for cash.
Punk became a fashion just like hippy used to be,
    and it ain't got a thing to do with you or me.

Movements are systems and systems kill.
    Movements are expressions of the public will.
Punk became a movement 'cos we all felt lost,
    but the leaders sold out and now we all pay the cost.
Punk narcissism was a social napalm,
    Johnny Rotten started doing real harm,
preaching revolution, anarchy and change
    as he sucked from the system that had given him his name.

Well I'm tired of looking through shit-stained glass,
    tired of staring up a superstar's arse,
I've got an arse and crap and a name,
    I'm just waiting for my fifteen minutes fame.
Johnny Rotten you're napalm,
    if you're so pretty vacant why do you smarm?
Patti Smith, you're napalm,
    you write with your hand, but it's Rimbaud's arm.

And me, yes, I, do I want to burn?

    Is there something I can learn?

Do I need a businessman to promote my angle?

    Can I resist the carrots that fame and fortune dangle?

I see the velvet zippies in their bondage gear,

    the social élite with safety-pins in their ear,

I watch and understand that it don't mean a thing,

    the scorpions might attack, but the system stole the sting.

                PUNK IS DEAD.

                PUNK IS DEAD.

                PUNK IS DEAD.

                PUNK IS DEAD.

1978

NAGASAKI NIGHTMARE

THEY'RE ALWAYS THERE HIGH IN THE SKIES...
    Nagasaki nightmare,
pretty as a picture in the general's eyes.
They've done it once, they'll do it again,
they'll shower us all in their deadly rain.

Fishing children fish in the Imperial Waters:
sons and lovers, lovers and daughters.
Cherry blossom hanging on the cherry blossom tree;
flash, blinding flash, then there's nothing to see.

Dying they're still dying, one by one.
Darkness in the land of the land of the rising sun.
Lesson, learnt the lesson? No, 'cos no one really cares,
it's so easy to be silent, just to cover up your fears.

So they die in the nightmare, nightmare, nightmare,
and live with the nightmare, nightmare, nightmare.
Will you stand by and let it happen again?
Nightmare death in the deadly rain.

Live with the nightmare, nightmare, nightmare,
and die in the nightmare, nightmare, nightmare.
Nightmare come in deadly rain,
nightmare, nightmare, nightmare rain.

Man-made power, man-made pain,
deadly rain, deadly rain.
They'll do it again, shower us in rain,
deadly, deadly, deadly rain. Nagasaki nightmare.

DARLING

EVE LIBERTINE

THEY SELL US LOVE AS DIVINITY,
when it's only a social obscenity.
Underneath we're all loveable.

Hello, hero, hero, hello.
Hello, hero, hello, hello.
Hello, hero, hero, hello.
Hello, hero, hero, hello.
Hello, hello, hello, hello.

Obscene sentimental, hero, hello.
Obsession, obsession, hello, hello.
Desire for protection, hero, hello.
Protect your possession, Enola, hello.
Possession, possession, hero, hello.
Protect your obsession, hero, hello.
Obsession, obsession, hello, hello.
Obscene sentimental, hero, hello.

Obscene sentimental, obsession, obsession.
Desire for protection, protect your possession.
Possession, possession, protect your obsession.
Obsession, obsession, obscene sentimental.
Protection, protection.

1979

MOTHER EARTH

PENNY RIMBAUD

MOTHER? MOTHER? MOTHER?

> She's the anti-mother,
> mother? Is that you?
> She's the anti-mother,
> mother? Mother is that you?

It's Myra Hindley on the cover,
    your very own sweet anti-mother.
There she is on the pages of *The Star*,
    ain't that just the place you wish you were?
Let her rot in hell is what you said,
    let her rot, let her starve, you'd see her dead.

Let her out, but don't forget to tell you where she is,
    the chance to screw her is a chance you wouldn't miss.
Let her suffer, give her pain is the verdict you gave,
    you just can't wait to piss on her grave.
You pretend that you're horrified, make out that you care,
    but really you wish that you had been there.
You say you can't bear the thought of what she did,
    but you'd do it to her, you'd see her dead.

Tell me, what is the difference between her and you?
You say that you would kill her, well, what else would you do?
Don't you see that violence has no end? Isn't limited by rules?
Don't you see as angels preaching, you're nothing but the fools?

1979

[132]

Fools step in where angels fear to tread,
     you see, to kill others is the ethic of the dead.

         She's the anti-mother,
         mother? Is that you?
         She's the anti-mother,
         mother? Mother is that you?

That single mug-shot from the past
     ensures your fantasy can last and last,
it gives you the chance to air your hate
     because she got there first, you were too late.
Hindley's crime was to do what others think,
     took her anger and her prejudice and pushed it to the brink.
Then you goodly Christian people, with your sickly mask of love,
     would tear that woman limb from limb.
You never get enough.

So you keep the story alive
     so you can make yourselves believe
that you are so much better than her,
     but you aren't, that's YOUR GUILT laying there.

1979

MOTHER LOVE

STEVE IGNORANT

MUMMY AND DADDY OWNED ME 'TIL I COULD UNDERSTAND,
that at the end of my arm was my own fucking hand,
that in my head I had a brain that they filled up with lies,
that I didn't fucking need them with their love and family ties.

Little children shouldn't speak until they're spoken to,
they're just another showpiece to show the neighbours who
can produce the perfect babe with everything in place,
but God help you if you come out with an angel face.

If you haven't got the looks that prove how nice you are,
you'll have failed your duty and that's all you fucking are,
you're just a status symbol that they need to have in life,
just the proof they need to be the perfect man and wife.

Mummy and daddy owned me 'til I could understand,
that at the end of my arm was my own fucking hand,
that in my head I had a brain that they filled up with lies,
that I didn't fucking need them with their love and family ties.

Just like a fucking dustbin they fill you up with trash,
and tell you all that life is, is working for some cash.
Life's a competition and you've got to be the best,
so tread on everybody else, forget about the rest.

1982

They tell you to be grateful for what they've done to you,
like tell you the conditions and pump it into you,
that you really mustn't fail them 'cos you owe them a debt,
'cos they're the ones that made you and they won't let you forget.

Mummy and daddy owned me 'til I could understand,
that at the end of my arm was my own fucking hand,
that in my head I had a brain that they filled up with lies,
that I didn't fucking need them with their love and family ties.

You're not a human in their eyes, you're a novelty.
They don't want you thinking 'cos you'll break the fantasy,
the fantasy that you're the toy providing endless fun.
You're not a human being, you're their daughter or their son.

You bring them lots of happiness when you're very small,
but when you lose those darling looks no-one cares to call,
'cos you're no more the cuddly toy for them to hug and hold,
you're not an individual and they're just getting old.

Mummy and daddy owned me 'til I could understand,
that at the end of my arm was my own fucking hand,
that in my head I had a brain that they filled up with lies.
Didn't fucking need them with their love and family ties.
Didn't fucking need them with their love and family ties.
Didn't fucking need them with their love and family ties.
Didn't fucking need them with their love and family ties.
Didn't fucking need them with their love and family ties.

1982

POISON IN A PRETTY PILL

JOY DE VIVRE

YOUR TACTILE EYES RUNNING OVER GLOSSY PAPER,
printed on with tactile lies of glaze and gauze.
They say, "forget yourself, adorn with this disguise";
this womanhood of smooth and tampered whores.
Let me warn you of their cold sensitivity,
they'll have you gathered in a trap of glass.
Is your reflection all that you will recognise?
That cruel lie will stare you in the face.
Wrapped up in haze and flow of bridal gown,
they tell your lover he must hold a gun.
You're the pornographic reassurance he's a man.
They deal in flesh, incarcerate with rags,
red lips, shimmer-silk and body-bags,
hairless legs against the blistered napalm burn.
I want to rape the substance of your downy hair,
in that mist a gutted child fights for air.

Against the fragile, mashed and sweaty wound,
your facile beauty has an outrageous sound,
like a glamour billboard on a battlefield.
At least the blood-red poppy was of nature's will.
That flower perfecting by the barbed wire fence
must be insulted by your scented poor pretence,
just as I, who finds it hard to touch you now,
you traumatise my love with needle doubts.
I want so gently to remove your mask.

1981

It's hard to enough to find water here,
in this barrenness of dishonesty and fear,
without you accepting poison in a pretty pill.
Your bandages on a bullet punctured corpse,
the layers of precious imitation worn,
are the layers of history that suffocate the unborn.

1981

OUR WEDDING

JOY DE VIVRE & PHIL FREE

ALL I AM I GIVE TO YOU,
you honour me I'll honour you.
Reaching for each other, come what may,
we'll forsake all other love.
Just we the two, one flesh one blood,
in the eyes of God.
I am yours to have and hold,
I'm giving you my life.
Never look at anyone, anyone but me,
never look at anyone, I must be all you see,
listen to those wedding bells,
say goodbye to other girls.
I'll never be untrue, my love,
don't be untrue to me ...
don't be untrue to me ...
don't be untrue to me ...
don't be untrue to me ...
don't be untrue to me ...
don't be untrue to me .

1981

Our Wedding was written and recorded as a satirical comment and then offered as a serious work to *Loving*, a teenage romance magazine. Having taken the bait, *Loving* offered it as a free flexi-disc in a special 'Brides' Issue', proclaiming it, *'a must for all true romantics'*.

BERKERTEX BRIBE

EVE LIBERTINE

THE OBJECT UNSOILED IS PACKED READY AND WAITING
for the moment of truth in this spiritual mating.
The object unsoiled is packed ready and waiting,
to be owned, to be cherished, to be fucked for the naming.

The public are shocked by the state of society,
but as for you, you're a breath of purity.
Well don't give me your morals, they're filth in my eyes,
you can pack them away with the rest of your lies.

Your painted mask of ugly perfection,
the ring on your finger, the sign of protection
is the rape on page three, is the soldiers obsession.
How well you've been caught to support your oppression.

     One god.
     One church.
     One husband.
     One wife.

Sordid sequences in brilliant life,
supports and props and punctuation
to our flowing realities and realisations.

We're talking with words that have been used before,
to describe us as goddesses, mothers and whores,
to describe us as women, describe us as men,

to set out the rules of this ludicrous game,
and it's all played very carefully, a delicate balance,
a masculine/feminine perfect alliance.

Does the winner take all?
What love in your grasping?
What vision is left and is anyone asking?
What vision is left and is anyone asking?

She's a Berkertex bride.
Bride.
BRIBE.

1982

SMASH THE MAC

PETE WRIGHT

Roll up, roll up to the land of dreams.
We weave and spin a web of fantasy.
We touch on the pain and fear,
then whisk you back to the consumer world,
touch the surfaces, smooth the veneer
while three-quarters of the world starves.
What do you care?
The glitter continuing to glitter,
the tinsel showers and Tinkerbell
waves the magic wand.
Sell sell, buy buy.
You know the name of the game...

— Penny Rimbaud

1984

ALL RIGHT, JACK, SITTING ON THE FENCE

They sit on the fence
real people stand against and say
they have the best intention.
Just a rip-off trick, it's always hip
to keep in with dissention.
And if an arms dealer is the record boss,
the record labels can run 'em at a loss.
It's money well spent to control the dross.
What they don't break gets bent... John.

All right, Jill, sitting on the fence.

The people are fooled by the parasites
who mindlessly entertain
and take rich pickings
from the bombed out crowds
who've paid to bury their pain,
while the clowns in the pantomine
don't give a toss, and sing about fucks
and fads and loss.
Sliding around in a genital froth,
our world slips down the drain.

That's really really wonderful,
well off the wall.
That's really really marvellous,
sitting on the fence,
really terrific, well out to lunch,
that really is a buzz, sitting on the fence.

Preening and posing in a life of pretence,
in a cynical mockery of caring,
well you can't see a turd in a barrel of shit
if that's their idea of sharing.
Yeah, peace is in, so dump an old track,
buy a little cred with the Greenham Pack,
the biz is keen to kill or catch,
as the people scream they're cheering

All right, Jack. All right, Jill.
The pen is mighty and looks can kill.
All right, Jack. All right, Jill.
In one hand a gift, in the other a bill.

1984

We've seen their best and we're not impressed,
so lets get priorities straight.
A hamper from Harrods and the patronising gestures
ain't gonna change the State.
While the people who care are prepared to act,
the pantomine clowns keep the system intact,
shamming a commitment they so obviously lack;
the love they sing is hate ... fakes

All right, Jack, shit on the fence.
All right, Jill, shit on the fence.

But the fence, the fence is owned by America,
sit on the fence owned by America,
they make no pretence, it's owned by America.
Jack and Jill on the fence, it's owned by America.

On their side American troopers and bombs,
on our side the trash and consumer cons.
We've been occupied, culture smashed and betrayed,
but the spirit is untouched ... look out ...

Smash the Mac, smash the Mac,
smash the Mac, smash the big Mac.

Bronco burgers, burnt out brain,
sterile fat, deadly rain,
chemical colours, Kentucky creams.
Cut your teeth on American ... dreams

Stickin' chicken American grains,
licking shittin' American reigns.

Kiddies fit in American trains.
Bombs tick in American ... planes

Smash the Mac, you're on your back.
Smash the Mac 'til it won't come back.

American tourist, American free,
two week tour in our misery.
A good museum, but a stinking home.
The natives hang on the rotten ... backbone

America owns, America wins,
comes in packets, bottles, tins.
Blinds our eyes, fills our ears,
it's been our soul for twenty ... years

Smash the Mac, American tack.
Smash the Mac, smash the big Mac.
Smash the Mac, make it crack.
Smash the Mac, smash the big Mac.

We stand among your war machines
looking for the light.
Squaddies, grunts and filth sip Pepsi-Cola,
wait to fight ...

The bricks of our world
that you cover in plastic
will sail through your plate-glass windows.

E.T. go home ...
E.T. go home ...
Mickey Mouse, fuck off.

1984

BATA MOTEL

EVE LIBERTINE

I'VE GOT FIVE, FOUR, THREE, TWO, ONE,
I've got a red pair of high-heels on.
Tumble me over, it doesn't take much,
tumble me over, tumble me, push.
In my red high-heels I've no control,
the rituals of repression are so old,
you can do what you like, there'll be no reprisal,
I'm yours, yes I'm yours, it's my means of survival.

I've got five, four, three, two, one,
come on my love, I know you're strong.
Push me hard, make me stagger,
the pain in my back just doesn't matter.
You force-hold me above the ground,
I can't get away, my feet are bound,
so I'm bound to say
that I'm bound to stay.

Today I look so good,
just like I know I should,
my breasts to tempt inside my bra,
my face is painted like a movie star.
I've studied my flaws in your reflection,
and put them to rights with savage correction.
I've turned my statuesque perfection
and shone it over in your direction.
So come on, darling, make me yours,
trip me over, show me the floor.

1981

Tease me, tease me, make me stay,
in my red high-heels I can't get away.
I'm trussed and bound like an oven ready bird,
but I bleed without dying and won't say a word.
Slice my flesh and I'll ride the scar,
put me into gear like your lady car.
Drive me fast and crash me crazy,
I'll rise from the wreckage as fresh as a daisy.
These wounds leave furrows as they heal,
I've travelled them, they're red and real,
I know them well, they're part of me,
my birth, my sex, my history,
they grew with me, my closest friend,
my pain's my own, my pain's my end.
Clip my wings so you know where I am,
I can't get lost while you're my man.
Tame me so I know your call,
I've stabbed my heels so I am tall,
I've bound my twisted falling fall,
beautiful mute against the wall,
beautifully mutilated as I crawl.
Use me, don't lose me.

I've got five, four, three, two, one,
I've got a red pair of high-heels on.
Strap my ankles, break my heels,
make me kneel, make me feel.
Turn, turn, turn, like a clockwork doll,
put in your key and give me a whirl.
Tease me, tease me, the reason to play,
in my red high-heels I can't get away.
I'll be your bonsai, your beautiful bonsai,

your black-eye bonsai, erotically rotting.
Will my tiny feet fit your desire?
Warped and tied I walk on fire.
Burn me out, twist my wrists,
I promise not to shout, beat me with your fists.
Squeeze me, squeeze me, make me feel,
in my red high-heels I'm an easy kill.
Tease me, tease me, make me see,
you're the only one, I need to be me.
Thankyou, will you take me?
Thankyou, will you make me?
Thankyou, will you break me?
Use me, don't lose so me,
Taste me, don't waste me.
Use, lose, taste, waste.

1981

DON'T GET CAUGHT

PETE WRIGHT

THEY WON'T FUCKING LISTEN.
We know our enemy,
they're hiding underground,
they want us to live and die in the shit they leave around.

What can we do,
what can we say,
we're not dead yet, to show we're alive?
The government says 'shove it' and 'don't get in the way',
but we're sliding down corpses on a world nose-dive.

People here cling tightly to their fear and their fun,
the dead are abroad, so our streets are clean,
even those who know it hide in *Sounds* and *Sun*.
What will it take to stop the machine?

It's only when we're serious and start to make a fuss
that the the smug politicians show their real face.
It's the copper and the squaddy who were once one of us,
now trained to do the the dirty work and know their place.

If they won't listen either, what can we do?
They're people, yes, but only people oppress.
If we have to go round them, we'll have to go through.
If it rains and there's no shelter we must work in the mess.

1984

They say they're only trying to uphold the law
and if they were off duty, we could talk some more.
OK, they're individuals, but when they're in a mob
they're under orders, it's a dirty job.
The Plods are taught to go for your neck
or bust your nose running their gauntlet.
PC Punishment on the spot,
take the law in their own hands and fuck us lot.
If we choose to leave the paths that we've been taught,
don't expect help, so don't get caught.

They try so very hard to seem reasonable and straight
and asked you twice to co-operate.
> *"You have every right to protest like anyone these days,*
> *but keep to the footpath and out the fucking way, see?"*
If you care enough to break the law,
just wait and see what you've got in store.
Poked up the arse and kicked in a cell,
you call for help, but go to hell.
If we choose to leave the paths that we've been taught,
don't expect help, so don't get caught.

Now take it easy, watch the *News At Ten*,
see the commie-anar-fems are at it again,
annoying the police and the passive 'grass roots'.
We're living in a country where the army shoots.
People with courage dumped and stranded,
don'ts and won'ts look-on empty-handed.
If you fuck-up the State, don't be a star,
they're stuck if they don't know who you are.
If we choose to leave the paths that we've been taught,
don't expect help, so don't get caught.

1984

To stand up for the good of all and make demands for peace
will bring us hard and sharp against the army and police.
Well, they're the poor too, just like us. Maybe it's too late,
the rich are in their bunker, the poor are at the gate.
Use our head to avoid confrontation,
our love to avoid exploitation.
If the uniforms choose to stay,
they'll have to learn to get out the fucking way.
If we choose to leave the paths we've been taught,
we cease to be the seeker, we become the sought.

. . .

*Inasmuch as the grand social circus has been
created through the forced labour of the people;
so, by our labours, will it be destroyed.*

– Penny Rimbaud

1984

SYSTEMATIC DEATH

PENNY RIMBAUD

SYSTEM, SYSTEM, SYSTEM,
death in life.
System, system, system,
the surgeon's knife.
System, system, system,
hacking at the chord.
System, system, system,
a child is born.
Poor little fucker, poor little kid,
never asked for life, no she never did.
Poor little baby, poor little mite,
crying out for food as her parents fight.

Send him to school.
Force him to crawl.
Teach him how to cheat.
Kick him off his feet.
Poor little schoolboy, poor little lad,
they'll pat him if he's good, beat him if he's bad.
Poor little kiddy, poor little chap,
they'll force feed his mind with their useless crap.

They'll teach her how to cook,
teach her how to look.
They'll teach her all the tricks,
create another victim for their greasy pricks.

1981

Poor little girly, poor little wench,
another little object to prod and pinch.
Poor little sweety, poor little filly,
they'll fuck her mind so they can fuck her silly.

He's grown to be a man.
He's been taught to fit the plan.
Forty years of jobs,
pushing buttons, pulling knobs.
Poor fucking worker, poor little serf,
working like a mule for half of what he's worth.
Poor fucking grafter, poor little gent,
working for the cash that he's already spent.

He's selling his life, she's his loyal wife,
timid as a mouse, she's got her little house.
He's got his little car and they share the cocktail bar.
She likes to cook his meals, you know, something that appeals.
Sometimes he work 'til late, so his supper has to wait,
but she doesn't really mind 'cos he's getting overtime.
He likes to put a bit away just for that rainy day,
'cos every little counts as the cost of living mounts.
Then they'd take a trip abroad, do all the things they can't afford.
She'd really like to have a fur, he'd like a bigger car.
They could buy a bungalow, with a Georgian door for show.
He might think of leaving work, but no, he wouldn't like to shirk.
He'd much prefer to stay and get his honest day's pay.
He's got a life of work ahead, there's no rest for the dead.
She's tried to make it nice.
He's said thankyou once or twice.

Deprived of any hope.
Taught they couldn't cope.
Slaves right from the start,
'til death do them part.
Poor little fuckers, what a sorry pair,
had their lives stolen, but they didn't really care.
Poor little darlings, just your ordinary folks,
victims of the system and its cruel jokes.

The couple view the wreckage
	and dream of home sweet home,
They'd almost paid the mortgage,
	then the system dropped it's bomb.

1981

THEY'VE GOT A BOMB

PETE WRIGHT

THEY WON'T DESTROY THE WORLD,
no they're not that crazy.
You're not dealing with the town-hall.
They're not crazy.
No political solution,
so why should we bother?
Well whose fucking head
do you think they're holding it over?

Four
Three
Two
One
FIRE ...

They can't wait to use it.
They can't wait to use it.
They can't wait to try it out.
They can't wait to use it.
They've got a bomb,
they've got a bomb,
and they can't wait to use it on me.

Twenty odd years now
waiting for the flash ...

1978

… all of the odd-balls
thinking we'll be ash.
Well the four-minute warning
has run on into years.
Are we waiting for them
to confirm our fears?

Four
Three
Two
One
FIRE …

They can't wait to use it.
They can't wait to use it.
They can't wait to try it out.
They can't wait to use it.
They've got a bomb,
they've got a bomb,
and they can't wait to use it on me.

They can build them small,
call it tactical,
stop the fall-out,
make it practical
to smash the misfits
who foul up their scene
with the practical, tactical,
killing machine.

1978

Four
Three
Two
One
FIRE ...

They can't wait to use it.
They can't wait to use it.
They can't wait to try it out.
They can't wait to use it.
They've got a bomb,
they've got a bomb,
and they can't wait to use it on me.

1978

SENTIMENT
(WHITE FEATHERS)

JOY DE VIVRE

FEATHERS BURN SO EASILY,
the cat is blinded in the garden,
last vision, the lark is flame.

The cattle-shed gives off the smell of Sunday kitchen,
the gentle eye, the dispensable perfection.

Before the flash take two weeks' food,
pile the sacks of earth and hide.

All of us here know it, we grew with it,
we grew it.

Fighting amongst ourselves,
leaving bits of flesh on barbed wire,
a little blood on the floor.

Locks and bars across the door,
well versed in violation,
our children beat each other in the garden.

Our failure to accept the earth;
we talk of love but push it to the edge.

1982

[158]

This is no natural aggression composing death,
I am afraid for beauty when I see the fist,
the perfect hand that turns against itself,
the perfect hand that holds a gun or wields a butcher's blade
　　　or leads to death the used-up bull
　　　　　or incarcerates the hopeless fool
　　　　　　　or takes the forest with a single flame
　　　　　　　　　and leaves the nest an empty shell.

Humankind condemns the hunting beast,
　　　yet his own choice leaves behind such ragged meat.

The military dream of blood,
　　　their sweet wine flowing in the veins of men
　　　　　who work towards our bloody end.

They fly Enola gaily, give birth to this waiting ... waiting,
　　　give us the reality of our hatred,
　　　　　give the earth nothing.

Melting,
goats dead on the green,
dying lambs bleating by the wire ... three last days on the earth,
　　　I lay down to die in the grass.

1982

MAJOR GENERAL DESPAIR

PENNY RIMBAUD

WE'RE LOOKING FOR A BETTER WORLD BUT WHAT DO WE SEE?
Just hatred, poverty, aggression, misery.
So much money spent on war
when three-quarters of the world is so helplessly poor.

Major General Despair sits at his desk,
planning a new mode of attack,
he's quite unconcerned about chance or risk,
the Major General's a hard nut to crack.

Oh yes, he designs a cruise missile,
tactically sound, operationally OK,
while the starving crawl onto the deathpile,
they can't avoid their fate another day.

Attack on the mind, but he calls it defence,
but I ask you again who's it for?
Do the starving millions who don't stand a chance
hope to benefit by his stupid war?

Babies crippled with hunger before they could walk,
mothers with dry breasts cry dry tears,
and meanwhile Major General Despair gives a talk
on increasing the war budget over the years.

How can they do it, these men of steel,
how can they plot destruction, pain?

1982

Is it the only way they can feel,
by killing again and again?

Is it some part of themselves that has died
that permits them to plan as they do?
Or is it us that is dead?
Do we simply hide from the responsibility to stop what they do?

There's so many of us, yet we let them have their way,
at this moment they're plotting and planning.
We've got to rise up to take their power away,
to save the world that they're ruining.

They're destroying the world with their maggot-filled heads:
death, pain and mutilation.
They've got the responsibility of millions of dead,
yet they're still bent on destruction.

The generals and politicians who advocate war
should be made to wade in the truth of it,
they should spend sleepless nights shivering with fear
and by daytime should crawl in the deathpit.

They'll find the truth of what they've done there,
festering corpses they and their kind made,
eyeless skulls that endlessly stare
having seen the truth of military trade.

The earth was our home, the wind and the air,
the blue sky, the grass and the trees,
but these masters of war, what do they care?
Only sentiments, these.

1982

It's our world, but through violence they took it away,
took dignity, happiness, pride.
They took all the colours and changed them to grey
with the bodies of millions that died.

They destroy real meaning through their stupid games,
make life a trial of fear.
They destroy what values we have with their aims,
make us feel it's wrong if we care.

Well, we do care, it's our home, they've been at it too long,
if it's a fight they want, it's beginning.
Throughout history we've been expected to sing their tired song,
but now it's OUR turn to lead the singing ...

Fight war not wars,
make peace not wars,
fight war not wars,
make peace not wars ...

1982

ONE, TWO, THREE, FOUR ... WE DON'T WANT YOUR FUCKING WAR.
ONE, TWO, THREE, FOUR ... WE DON'T WANT YOUR FUCKING WAR.
ONE, TWO, THREE, FOUR ... WE DON'T WANT YOUR FUCKING WAR.
ONE, TWO, THREE, FOUR ... WE DON'T WANT YOUR FUCKING WAR.

FIGHT WAR, NOT WARS

PENNY RIMBAUD

FIGHT WAR, NOT WARS,
fight war, not wars,
fight war, not wars,
fight war, not wars,
fight war, not wars,
fight war, not wars,
fight war, not wars,
fight war, not wars,
fight war, not wars,
fight war, not wars,
fight war, not wars,
fight war, not wars,
fight war, not wars,
fight war, not wars,
fight war, not wars,
fight war, not wars,
fight war, not wars,
fight war, not wars,
fight war, not wars,
fight war, not wars,
fight war, not wars,
fight war, not wars,
fight war, not wars,
fight war, not wars,
fight war, not wars ...

DEMONCRATS

PENNY RIMBAUD

I AM NOT HE, NOR MASTER, NOR LORD;
no crown to wear, no cross to bear in stations.

I am not he, nor shall be
warlord of nations.

These heroes have run before me,
now dead upon the flesh-piles, see?

Waiting for their promised resurrection.
There is none.

Nothing but the marker, crown or cross
in stone upon these graves.

Promise of the ribbon was all it took,
where only the strap would leave its mark upon these slaves.

What flag to thrust into this flesh,
rag, bandage, mop in their flowing death?

Taken aside, they were pointed a way,
for God, Queen and Country. Now in silence they lie.

They ran before these masters, children of sorrow,
as slaves to that trilogy they had no future.

1979

They believed in democracy, freedom of speech,
yet dead on the flesh piles I hear no breath,
I hear no hope, no whisper of faith,
from those that have died for some others' privilege.

Out from your palaces, princes and queens,
out from your churches, you clergy, you Christs,
I'll neither live nor die for your dreams.

I'll make no subscription to your paradise.
I'll make no subscription to your paradise.
I'll make no subscription to your paradise.
I'll make no subscription to your paradise.
I'll make no subscription to your paradise.
I'll make no subscription to your paradise.
I'll make no subscription to your paradise.
I'll make no subscription to your paradise.
I'll make no subscription to your paradise.
I'll make no subscription to your paradise.
I'll make no subscription to your paradise.
I'll make no subscription to your paradise.
I'll make no subscription to your paradise.
I'll make no subscription to your paradise.
I'll make no subscription to your paradise.
I'll make no subscription to your paradise.
I'll make no subscription to your paradise.
I'll make no subscription to your paradise.
I'll make no subscription to your paradise.
I'll make no subscription to your paradise.
I'll make no subscription to your paradise.
I'll make no subscription to your paradise.

1979

CONTAMINATIONAL POWER

GEE VAUCHER

CAUSE A DISTURBANCE, DON'T LET THIS SLIDE BY,
do you want to end up a McDonald's french fry?
Atomic power, atomic power, death shower, Maggie's power.

The dust is settling, ticking in your brain,
ain't imagination gonna blow you away.
Who cares a fuck as it's work for the people?
Compromised labour you build your death with.
Cheaper goodies, more time with the family?
Don't be fooled with their gesture of equality.
The only thing that's equal is your own rotting corpse,
staring at each other to see who'll make it first.

Cause a disturbance, don't let this slide by,
do you want to end up a McDonald's french fry?
Atomic power, atomic power, death shower, Maggie's power.

She holds it over you, you won't hear a thing,
no great contender to help the people win.
Another White Paper gets waved in the air,
a victory for the modern world, but you won't be there.
Are you gonna let it shower over you?
The new great energy that sucks off yours,
giving all you wanted as it settles in your pores.
Make it known just this once that people ain't toys.

1979

Cause a disturbance, cause a fucking noise,
atomic power is just another of their ploys,
to build their firepower and defend the nation,
they expose us to contamination.

Contamination, contamination, contamination,
contamination, contamination, contamination,
contains the nation, that old sensation.
Contamination, contamination, contamination,
contamination, contamination, contamination.
Cause a disturbance, cause a fucking noise,
atomic power is just another of their ploys
TO BLOW YOU RIGHT AWAY.

1979

SO WHAT?

STEVE IGNORANT

THEY ASK ME WHY I'M HATEFUL, WHY I'M BAD,
they tell me I got things they never had,
they tell me go to church and see the light,
'cos the good Lord's always right.

Well, so what, so what?

So what if Jesus died on the cross?
So what about the fucker? I don't give a toss.
So what if the Master walked on the water?
I don't see him trying to stop the slaughter.

They say I wouldn't have to live from bins,
if I would go along, confess my sins.
They say I shouldn't commit no crime,
'cos Jesus Christ is watching all the time.

So what, so what?

So what if he's always over my shoulder?
I realise the truth as I get older,
I get to see what a con it is,
because it's my life, mine not his.

Well, they say they're going to send me away,
said they're going to make me pay.

1978

We're sorry but you have to go.
You were naughty, you said "No".
So what, so what?

So what if I see through the lies?
So what if the people I despise
twist my arm and make me work?
I'm no deaf, dumb fucking jerk,
I'm no spastic lying in the street,
I'm no superstar élite.
I'm just a person, a human being.

NO YOU'RE NOT, YOU'RE A PART OF OUR MACHINE

You're a part of our machine because we want you to be.
We've got you now and you'll never be free.
We can even have your body after you're dead.
We can take the eyes out of your fucking head,
we can take them out, use them again.
We can do it you know, 'cos we've got your brain.

We'll crucify you like we crucified him.
We'll make you obey our every whim.
We got the power, the power and the glory.
I've heard that before in a different story,
but the story I heard covered up the truth,
didn't touch on the actual factual truth,
didn't say about the bodies in the concentration camps,
didn't say about the surgeons' knives underneath the lamps,
doesn't say that the ovens are still warm,
doesn't say that this wretched little form,
is a human being who wants to live,
but not in the snot and shit they give.

They say that I had better keep quiet,
or they're gonna douse my light;
Jesus Christ can save my life.
But I can always use the knife.

So what?
So what?
So what?
So what?
So what?
So what?
SO WHAT?

1978

SYSTEM

PETE WRIGHT

YOU CAN SWEAR BY WHO THE FUCK YOU LIKE,
    but you're still on the roof.
I'm not gonna change the system,
they're not gonna change the system,
we're not gonna change the system.
Where does that leave you?
Where does that leave me?

Jumping up and down to a bunch of tools,
    the organisation treat us like fools.
They can't help it, they didn't make the rules,
    it's just the system again. BOLLOCKS.
Bind us round with ignorance,
    fit us up with a petty stance.
Fill us up with cheap romance,
    leave no option, no chance.
What've they got?
Fuck all? NO.
What've they got?
A swimming pool.
Where did they get it?
Follow the rules.
System, system, system.

Keeping their fingers on the breaks,
    down the ladders, up the snakes.
Buy the band and call the tune. Nah. Nah, nah, nah, nah.

BIG MAN, BIG M.A.N.

PENNY RIMBAUD

THEY'RE TELLING YOU TO DO IT,
  grow up and toe the line.
They tell you if you do it,
  everything will turn out fine.
Oh yes, oh yes, oh yes, what a wonderful lie,
  God, Queen and Country, colour telly and wife.

It's great if you can do it, it doesn't take a lot,
  just means you must destroy what sensitivity you've got.
Well, that's an easy bargain for the things you're going to get.
You can treat the wife like shit, own a car, a telly set,
  slip off in the evenings for a little on the sly,
    and if the wife complains, fuck her first,
      then black her eye.

There's lots of worthwhile jobs for the lad who wants to know.
Lorry driving's fun, you're always on the go,
  one hand on the wheel, the other up some cunt,
    or jerking off to *Penthouse* with the motorway up front.

The police force offers chances for a bright intelligent lad,
  to interfere with anyone 'cos they're there just to be had.
It offers quite a range for aggression and for spite,
  to take out your frustrations in a justifiable light.

1979

It's a mans' life in the army, good pay and lots of fun,
    you can stab them with your bayonet,
        fuck them with your gun.
Look smart in your uniform, that always pulls the skirt,
    then when you've fucked them good and proper,
        tell them they're just dirt.

'Cos man is spelt big M.A.N., it's the letters of the law.
Man is spelt big M.A.N., that's who the law is for.
You see there's lots of chances in this land of hope and glory,
    but try and make your own rules, that's a different story.
If you're a man, you'd better act like one,
    develop your muscles, use your prick like a gun,
        fuck anything that moves, but never pay the price.
Steal, fuck, slaughter, that's their advice.
Are you man enough? ask the posters on the walls,
    have you got what it takes? Guts and balls?

Keep your myth of manhood, it's been going on too long,
    a history of slaughter is the proof that it is wrong.

        Big man, big M.A.N.
        Big man, big M.A.N. Big wrong.
        Big man, big M.A.N.
        Big man, big M.A.N.
        Big man, J.O.K.E.
        Big man, what a fucking joke.

1979

HEALTH SURFACE

JOY DE VIVRE

PLACES OF SICKNESS NURSE ME COLD,
attendant whiteness glare in dark,
straighten out the winding sheet
twisted round in poorest dreams.

Shattered proofing of the lost,
splinter shackled, little wounds
of cruelty and truth, they tie
the one way sickness up inside.

Regressive smile, a baby's laugh,
a learnt contortion of the mouth.
Places of laughter leave me cool,
hot fire dying down to ash.

Beauty breezes through so swift,
endless roundabout of grief.
Not much to ask, a rightful place
where nothing matters, but can touch.

Without a sinking heart, this sigh
could be the wind among the leaves.
This pain does not belong to me,
they've taken everything away.

1981

To nurse the sicknesses of loss,
instilled with fear and bleachy guilt,
impatient winds up in her cloth,
the tired shoes are splitting up.

With weighty promises of love,
waiting for the last to fall away.
Buckle noose around the strap,
all that separates the flesh.

From green grass or sinking mud,
stagnating, knowing the delusion,
clean sheets waiting for a body,
slapped into life and slowly gutted.
A place of sickness is to die in.
Tired of the cruelty and lying,
drip-fed tears of the forsaken.
They say, "We'll soon have you up and walking".
Took the prison for a stronghold.
Took the lies for a love-song.
Paid for life on a shoestring.

Waiting for the last to fall away.
Buckle noose around the strap,
all that separates the flesh,
from green grass or sinking mud ...

THEY'VE GOT BIG HANDS

EVE LIBERTINE

OUT OF THE CHAOS WE DIVIDE,
    fucked up, muddled up, looking for a side.
Stay on the outside, don't go in,
    don't think that you can do it, if you sell-out they win.
It's not like that the changes are made,
    give in to them, your chances are delayed.
You'll feed with your energies the things that you hate,
    diluting your strength each time they say "yes".

Their hands are big, they've got big hands,
    big hands, big hands, big hands.

You're talking with sounds they don't understand:
    big hands, big hands, big hands.
They've got big mouths to shout demands:
    big hands, big hands, big hands.
You think you're getting somewhere, you're fucking blind:
    big hands, big hands, big hands.
This structure stretches, it'll bend, but not break:
    big hands, big hands, big hands.
This system channels any threat that you make:
    big hands, big hands, big hands.

1979

It will do almost anything to accommodate,
  accommodate you and your liberal ideas.
You're the child in their garden, the dog on their lead,
  their token to changes that are never made.
Can't you see that for centuries it's been the same,
  plenty like you been seduced to the game?
The chain's still as tight,
  won't let in the light.
Can you tell me what's different?
Whose hope you will feed?
Will you feed their arses?
    Will you feed their hands?
      Big hands, big hands, big hands,
      big hands, big hands, big hands.

1979

TIRED

PETE WRIGHT

WHAT DO YOU WANT?
What do you want?

I'm tired of adrenaline soaked fools,
tired of idiots playing with the rules,
know it's not a thing that a man would do,
but you get the same rush by jumping a bus queue.

Tired of bully boys looking for a fight,
I'm not a hard nut, so stuff it, right?
They really got you in a down-trodden state,
hopelessly, endlessly, heavily, totally straight.

What do you want?
What do you want?

I'm tired of playing with vice,
tired of hash heads trying to be nice.
Do you feel insulted when they pull out the dope?
Synthetic togetherness, token for a toke.

Do you get a buzz when you reminisce?
"Too much man, it was better than this."
I don't want a relativity talk,
if that's the bus ride, I think I'd rather walk.

1979

What do you want?
What do you want?

I don't want it, you can take it back,
I don't want to face another attack.
Shits all running round looking for a crack,
want another corpse to put on the stack.

What do you want?
What do you want?

1979

RIVAL TRIBAL REBEL REVEL

PENNY RIMBAUD

COR BLIMEY GUVNOR I'M THE BIG 'UN,
cop an eyeful of this muscular arm.
Doling out pain is my kind of fun.
Get my drift? I mean real harm.
I like the sound of cracking bones.
At the sight of blood I thrill.
I like to listen to the agonised moans
as I go in for the kill.

Tribal wars are raging,
there's a battlefield in the street.
There's games to play and hell to pay
when the rival tribal rebels meet.

I'd rip anybody limb from limb, you see,
skivvy and chivvy them through.
I'll simply DO any bastard who ain't like me,
there's no telling what, why or who.
I ain't got a purpose and I don't give a fuck,
I never asked for this life.
If you're looking for reasons, you're out of luck,
I'll show you the point with my knife.

Tribal wars are raging,
no-one's safe out on their own.
The gangs are about and they scream and shout,
so you'd better not be caught alone.

1980

I do it 'cos there ain't nothing else to do,
nowhere'll let me in.
I love to hate, to hurt, to screw,
so I've destroyed every place where I've been.

Smashed up the local so I can't get a beer,
at the dancehall I chivvied up this bloke,
left him with a smile cut from ear to ear,
but the bleeder never got the joke.

Once I had a bird, but I put her up the spout,
so I told her where she could get off.
She cried a bit, said I was a lout,
but if you're a man you've got to be tough.

I used to go down the cafe for tea,
but I put me boot through the door,
so now it ain't open for the likes of me,
and I'm back on the streets like before.

Tribal wars are raging,
our heroes are standing tall,
but the truth of the matter if you cut out the patter
is that pride comes before a fall.

They can stand on their corner with their violence and their hate,
stand there and fester 'til they've left it too late
to realise it's themselves that they've put there on the spot,
'cos they've wasted the one and only life that they've got.

Tribal wars are raging,
everyone's just acting out bad parts.
Hey there, big man, take a look at yourself,
it's in the mirror that the real war starts.

CRUTCH OF SOCIETY

GEE VAUCHER

DON'T WANT TO BURY MY HEAD IN THE CRUTCH OF SOCIETY,
perverted parent that takes my energy,
sucking me dry with your morals, your threats,
Christ, your Queen, your politics.

Fucking hypersensitive, super-realist humanity,
I'm one of your super hybrid community,
commutes the arsehole of the economy.

Watch out, watch out, it's all about,
reversion's setting in,
and I can see you,
staring at me with your seizured brain,
trying to put me down the drain again.

Well you're too smart, right from the start
I learned it well that the truth will tell,
and you're done for,
it's what the son's for,
that's what the gun's for,
it's what I come for.
You better run bore,
you better run bore.

1979

THE GASMAN COMETH

PENNY RIMBAUD

WHAT WILL YOU DO WHEN THE GAS TAPS TURN?
Where will you be when the bodies burn?
Will you just watch as the cattle trucks roll by?
Pretend it isn't happening? Turn a blind eye?
Have you seen the army convoys quietly passing by?
Heard the helicopters in your little bit of sky?
Have you seen the squad-cars packed with boys in blue?
Have you ever wondered what they're there to do?

Pictures in the papers of soldiers in the street,
pictures in the history books of rotting human meat.
Auschwitz's now a tourist spot for the goggle-eyed to pry,
still in working order for you and I.
Photos of the victims, of gas, of gun, of bomb,
inheritance of violence in the bookshelves of your home.
Don't wait for it to come to you, 'cos come it surely will,
the guardians of the State are trained to search, destroy and kill.

There's people sitting at this moment, fingers on the trigger,
there's loyalty and royalty to make their violence figure.
"Allegiance to the flag," they say, as they lock the prison door,
allegiance to normality, that's what lobotomies are for.
God, Queen and Country, they say we've got the choice,
free speech for all if you've got no voice.
Propaganda on the airwaves, here's the way to live,
it's not for you and me the alternative.

They look for peace in Ireland with a thousand squaddy boys.
Torture in their mental homes is another of their ploys.
They'll keep us all in line, by Christ, they'll keep us on our toes,
but if we stand against their power, we'll see how violence grows.
Read it in the paper about rebellious youth,
but it's them that are so violent, it's them that hide the truth.
Stay in line, or pay the cost,
do you think they care when another life's lost?

To ashes at Auschwitz it's just a small leap
from coshes at Southall. Life is cheap.
Don't think that they won't do it, 'cos they already do,
but this time round the pawns are me and you.

1979

DEADHEAD

PETE WRIGHT

TIRED BORED SAD PEOPLE, TIRED BORED SAD LIVES,
endless cars on endless roadways past endless shopfronts
        with endless lies.
Even the winners, even the punters, tight-lipped packages,
        think it's bad.
Can't imagine a revolution could deal with anything so sad.
Well it's all set up so you can't do it,
no let up so you don't make it
and all arranged so you can't have it,
all enclosed so you won't take it.
Set in little pockets of isolation,
separated by regulation,
crushed for product in a rich man's passion,
relative ration for the ration nation.
Tear a bit, smash a bit, cause a little pain,
that's a contribution then they build it up again.
Fool yourself thinking it's a holy-held belief
when all the time it's just another light relief.
Oh boredom, psychological stunt,
you never really feel it when you're up at the front,
and it doesn't really matter where the hell it's going
as long as everybody has the hot blood flowing ...

Excitement and thrills
will put off the ills.
Radical frills.
Docility pills.

New Wave, splash in the pan,
real music by dildo dan.
Tired old discos, sham balam,
sodden modern, Christ, futurists again.
Play the machine,
crank up the dream.
We're just what we seem.
Know what I mean?

But no-one can wipe out the last five years,
so there's other ways of living than in Superglue pairs.
Marry me darling?
Fuck off, creep!
Tired and lonely, life on the cheap.
Didn't plan it, but now we're very happy.
Another poor fucker drowns in its nappy.
Bakunin and bollocks and fun and farts;
hit the right fantasy and come up the charts.

Treat people like shit and that's what you get.

1982

HEARD TOO MUCH ABOUT

GEE VAUCHER

I'VE HEARD TOO MUCH ABOUT THE PEOPLE IN THE GHETTO,
heard too much about the working-class motto.

How you don't know life if you ain't seen the street,
racialist poor against the racialist élite.

A million people in factory and office,
aware there's something missing, but living with their losses.

There's no fight to get where they'd rather be,
     only the accepting of dependency.
Wait in the shop, for what you ain't got,
     lying on the beaches for the social élite.
Working 9 to 4, revolved round more:
     fear, guilt, abuse, love and moral truth.
War in your bedroom, bodies in your fridge,
     domestic violence, the tomb you dig.

Rules for survival, rules that they wrote,
     thinking it's your freedom
          when it's rammed down your throat.
Choose your family, on the boundary,
     choose what school, no choice at all.
Choose what church, it allows you to hurt,
     choose your power is choosing your hour.

1979

THE GREATEST WORKING
CLASS RIP OFF

PENNY RIMBAUD

AIN'T IT JUST A RIP OFF? OI, OI, OI.
Ain't it just a rip off? Oi, oi, oi.
Ain't it just a rip off? Oi, oi, oi.
What a fucking rip off: oi, oi, oi.

Another threatening glance, another macho stance,
another aggressive fist, another arsehole pissed,
another vicious threat, a stream of blood-stained sweat,
another bottle waved in the air,
      another battle with tension and fear.

Ain't it just a rip off? Oi, oi, oi.
Ain't it just a rip off? Oi, oi, oi.
Ain't it just a rip off? Oi, oi, oi.
What a fucking rip off: oi, oi, oi.

Tell me, why do you glorify violence?
      Ain't there nothing better to give?
Why fuck up the only chance to be yourself and really live?
You tell me you're a working-class loser,
      well what the fuck does that mean?
Is the weekly fight at the boozer
      gonna be the only action you've seen?
Are you gonna be one of the big boys? Well, we've seen it all before,
muscles all akimbo as they boot down another door.
Will you see yourself as the hero as you boot in another head,
when you're just a pathetic victim of the media you've been fed?

You're lost in your own self pity, you've bought the system's lie.
They box us up and sit pretty
      as we struggle with the knots they tie.
Okay, so you're right about one thing,
      no-one's got the right to shit on you,
but what's the point of shitting on yourself, what's that gonna do?
Working-class hero beats up middle-class twit:
media labels, system's shit.
When it looks like the people could score a win,
the system makes sure that the boot goes in.

Yeah, it's the greatest working-class rip off: oi, oi, oi,
just another fucking rip off, a fucking media ploy.
It's the greatest working-class rip off: oi, oi, oi.
Ain't it just a rip off? Ain't it just a rip off, ain't it just a rip off? Oi.

Punk attacked the barriers of colour, class and creed,
      but look at how it is right now, do you really think you're freed?
Punk once stood for freedom, not violence, greed and hate.
Punk's got nothing to do with what you're trying to create.
Anarchy, violence, chaos?
You mindless fucking jerks,
can't you see you're talking about the way the system works?
Throughout our bloody history, force has been the game,
the message that you offer is just the fucking same.
You're puppets to the system with your mindless violent stance.
That's right, you fuckers, sneer at us 'cos we say
      "Give Peace a chance."
Punk is dead, you wankers, 'cos you killed it through and through.
In your violent world of chaos, what you gonna do?
Is *Top of the Pops* the way in which you show
      how much you care?

Will you take off now to the USA to spread your message there?
Well, mouth and trousers, sonny boy, never changed a thing,
the only thing that'll ever change will be the song you sing,
'cos when you've bought your Rolls Royce car
        and luxury penthouse flat,
you'll be looking down your nose and saying
        "Punk, dear chap, what's that?"
You'll be the working-class hero with your middle-class dream,
and the world will be the same as the world has always been.
Punk's the people's music, so you can stuff ideas of class,
that's just the way the system keeps you sitting on your arse.
Class, class, class, that's all you fucking hear;
middle-class? working-class? I don't fucking care.

It's the greatest working class rip off: oi, oi, oi.
What a fucking rip off: oi, oi, oi.
It's the greatest human sell off: oi, oi, oi.
Ain't it just a rip off? Oi, oi, oi.

Punk's the people's music and I don't care where they're from,
black or white, punk or skin, there ain't no right or wrong.
We're all just human beings, some of us rotten, some of us good,
you can stuff your false divisions 'cos together I know we could
beat the system, beat its rule,
ain't got no class, I ain't a fool.
Beat the system, beat its law,
ain't got no religion 'cos I know there's more.
Beat the system, beat its game,
ain't got no colour, we're all the same.
People, people, not colour, class or creed.
Don't destroy the people, destroy their power and their greed.

HURRY UP GARRY
(THE PARSON'S FARTED)

PENNY RIMBAUD

THE BASTARDS,
what are they playing at?
Don't like the music,
don't like the words,
don't like the sentiments.
Well keep it for the birds and bees, boys:
bastards.

Yes that's right,
I stepped out of line.
What do you want?
What do you want?
As long as I play it moderate,
that's fine. Well,
fuck off runt, fuck off runt.

Pick your nose with your ball pen, stick your snot in *Sounds*,
back to your play-pen with your street cred minds.
You whimper and whine from the pages of the press,
ridicule and criticise those that want to change this mess.
There's people out here who are trying to live,
people who care, now,
what do you give?

1979

So many parasites living off our sweat,
so many fuckers in it for what they can get.
Punk ain't about your standards and your rules,
it ain't another product for the suckers and the fools.
You sit behind your typewriters shovelling shit,
rotting in the decadence of your crap-lined pit,
waiting for the action so you can grab a part,
but it stinks so bad where you come from,
who's going to smell your fart?

"Can you put me on the guest list?
Is there any freebie drink?
I can't write unless I get pissed."

Piss off, you fucking stink.

1979

WHITE PUNKS ON HOPE

PENNY RIMBAUD

THEY SAID THAT WE WERE TRASH,
    well the name is Crass, not Clash.
They can stuff their punk credentials
    'cause it's them that take the cash.
They won't change nothing with their fashionable talk,
    their RAR badges and their protest walk.
Thousands of white men standing in a park
    objecting to racism is like a candle in the dark.
Black man's got his problems and his way to deal with it,
    so don't fool yourself you're helping
        with your white liberal shit.
If you care to take a closer look at the way things really stand,
    you'd see we're all just niggers to the rulers of this land.

Punk was once an answer to years of crap,
    a way of saying "no" where we'd always said "yep",
        but the moment we found a way to be free,
            they invented a dividing line: street credibility.
The qualifying factors are politics and class,
    left-wing macho street-fighters willing to kick arse.
They said because of racism they'd come out on the street,
    but it was just a form of fascism for the socialist élite.
Bigotry and blindness, a Marxist con,
    another clever trick to keep us all in line.
Neat little labels to keep us all apart,
    to keep us all divided when the troubles start.

Pogo on a Nazi, spit upon a Jew,
   vicious mindless violence that offers nothing new.
Left-wing violence, right-wing violence, all seems much the same,
   bully boys out fighting, it's just the same old game.
Boring fucking politics that'll get us all shot,
   left-wing, right-wing, you can stuff the lot.
Keep your petty prejudice, I don't see the point,
   ANARCHY AND FREEDOM IS WHAT I WANT.

1979

TIME OUT

GEE VAUCHER

THEY'RE USING SKATEBOARDS AS SPASTIC CHAIRS
for the legless fuckers who fought your affairs.
They're moulding babies' dummies with a permanent smile,
to put the bleeders early in rank and file.
They're giving you a chance to be a plastic wrap,
around the doggies' meat-can, full of fucking crap.
They're making little dollies, they tell you "it's a boy,"
baby brother, tender love, to bring you lots of joy.
They're making plastic families, all neighbourly folk,
so she can wash and dress them. What a fucking joke.

They're teaching little Johnny to shoot the gun,
"a terrific way," says father, "to get to know your son."
Spare parts, body parts, I'm somebody.
Ever seen the arms and legs of some poor squaddy?
There's signs in the food stores, advertising meat,
beef blade, chuck roast, last you all the week.
They're telling you you like it, you're saying that you do,
they don't have to force it and tell you how to chew.
You swallow it whole, without a fucking squeak,
sitting there quietly and up they creep.

You think you're fucking different, you think it's you and them,
if they asked you a question you'd ask them "when?".
You think you're hard done by, but you just want the same,
chicken thighs, human thighs, it's all the same old game.

1979

[195]

Well, you made the choice: money, sex and crime,
tight little egos asking for the time.
Well I ain't got it, you can sit in your pit,
    middle-class,
        working-class,
            it's all a load of shit.

1979

FUN GOING ON

PETE WRIGHT

MAYBE YOU THINK IT'S THE NEW, NEW WAVE,
when all it is is just another rave.

Maybe it looks like the writing on the wall,
but you've seen it before, it's another death pall.

So somebody's coming with the answer to the crap,
well it's just bad rock-and-roll chivvied up a bit.

Someone's looking after it, there's time for a laugh,
but you're leading yourself up the garden path.

A million people are sitting out of work,
I never wanted in, I'm treated as a shirk.

Who's the fool in the Irish joke,
when they say all you've got is your stupid vote?

It's all very comfy while they keep the war vocal,
but the bombs in Belfast are coming down your local.

I wanna know how much you can take,
'cos you've taken it all, and that's just great.

Go and see a band and it's another fucking bore,
another bunch of jerks are shitting on the poor.

Or you might just get the adrenaline rush,
or the jock-rot heavy-metal, leg-iron gush.

Avé fucking Maria is what I say,
she's still going strong and it won't go away.

You can run religion on a football chant,
or the other way around if that's what you want.

You can get anyone crawling through shit,
skivvying their lives away, slaving in the pit.

All you need is to have the right key,
comfort and justice and liberty.

Hi, mum, hi, dad, family life,
'til your heart blows up from those shitty lies.

Have some fun while you're young, son,
fun while you're young.

Fun fun fun, it's gonna go on.

SUCKS

PETE WRIGHT

DO YOU REALLY BELIEVE IN BUDDHA?
Buddha sucks.
Do you really believe in Jesus?
Jesus fucks.

Is it alright really?
Is it alright really?
Is it working?

Do you really believe in Marx?
Marx fucks.
Do you really believe in Thatcher?
Maggie sucks.

Is it alright really?
Is it alright really?
Is it working?

Do you really believe in the system?
Well, OK.
I BELIEVE IN ANARCHY IN THE UK.

Is it alright really?
Is it alright really?
Is it working?

1978

ANGELS

PENNY RIMBAUD

THE ANGELS ARE ON TV TONIGHT:
    grey puke, celluloid shit.
The army have sent a mission to Ireland,
    just to see to it.
Kojak is on the TV streets again:
    grey puke, fucking shit.
The army say they seek peace in Ireland,
    and they'll see to it ...

that they keep in line,	horizontal hold.
Keep in line,	vertical hold.
Keep in line,	brightness.
Keep in line,	contrast.
Keep in line,	VISION ON.

Coronation Street is on twice a week:
    grey puke, fucking shit.
The army say that they seek peace in Ireland,
    and that they'll see to it.
The army are on the news report:
    WARS. BULLETS. DEATH.
They're beating fuck out of someone,
    just to see to it ...

that they keep in line,	horizontal hold.
Keep in line,	vertical hold.
Keep in line,	brightness.
Keep in line,	contrast.
Keep in line,	VISION OFF.

1978

REJECT OF SOCIETY

STEVE IGNORANT

NOT FOR ME THE FACTORY FLOOR,
sweeping up from nine to four.
Not for me the silly rat race,
I don't see the point in any case.

People ask me why I say what I do,
I say to them, "Well wouldn't you
if you were fucked up just like me,
a reject of society?"

They say I dig a hole and jump right in.
Well I don't give a shit about anything.
I don't comply to their silly rules,
all they are is hypocritical fools.

You give us conscience money.
Now you start to worry.
The Frankenstein monster you created
has turned against you, now you're hated.

They tell me I'm not what they'd like me to be.
It's their fault, you can't blame me.
They fucking tricked me half the time,
now they've got to stand in line.

1978

They don't like it when they see me have fun,
they turn around and then they run.
They don't listen to what I say;
I'm a reject of society.

1978

END RESULT

STEVE IGNORANT

I AM A PRODUCT,
I am a symbol
of endless, hopeless, fruitless, aimless games.
I'm a glossy package on a supermarket shelf,
my contents aren't fit for human consumption.
I could tragically injure your perfect health,
my ingredients will seize up your body's function.
I am the dirt that everyone walks on.
I am the orphan nobody wants.
I am the stair-carpet everyone walks on.
I am the leper nobody wants
to touch ... much.

I am a sample,
I am a scapegoat
of useless, futureless, endless, mindless ideas.
I'm a number on the paper you file away.
I'm a portfolio you stick in a drawer.
I'm the fool you try to scare when you say
"We know all about you of that you can be sure".
Well I don't want your crazy system,
I don't wanna be on your files.
Your temptations I try to resist them
'cos I know what hides behind your smiles,
it's ... EST.

1978

I am a subject,
I am a topic
for useless, futureless, endless, mindless debates.
You think up ways that you can hide me
from the naïve eyes of your figurehead,
but don't you find that it ain't easy?
Wouldn't you love to see me dead?
Your answer is to give me treatment
for crying out when you give me pain,
leave me with no possible remnant,
you poke your knives into my brain.
You send me insane.

I'm an example,
I'm no hero
of the great, intelligent, magnificent, human race.
I'm part of the race that kills for possessions,
I'm part of the race that's wiping itself out,
I'm part of the race that's got crazy obsessions,
like locking people up, not letting them out.
I hate the living dead and their work in the factories,
they go like sheep to their production lines,
they live on illusions, don't face the realities.
All they live for is that big blue sign.
It says ... FORD.

I'M BORED, BORED, BORED.

1978

CHAIRMAN OF THE BORED

PENNY RIMBAUD

1979

TIRING MOMENTS, FUCKED UP MINDS,
empty faces, eyes that are blind.

Flick through the papers, car crash, death,
vacant pages offer no breath
of hope, future, possibility
to those fucked-up mindless people who haven't got the eyes to see
that the pages of *The Guardian* or the pages of *The Sun*
are just a load of fucking lies, are just a fucking con.

Why do they feed us rubbish?
Why do they feed us shit?
Is this really what they think we want?
Scrapings from the pit?

Why don't they give us something which isn't just their lies,
their own particular angle from their own unseeing eyes?

I'm the chairman of the bored,
and I'm asking for some truth.
I'm the chairman of the bored,
and I'm looking for some proof
that there's something more than their fucked-up game,
that their mindless lives and mine aren't the same.
I'm looking for something that I can call my own,
which ain't a Ford Cortina or a mortgage on a home.

I'm the chairman of the bored,
and I'm asking for some truth.
I'm the chairman of the bored,
and I'm looking for some proof.

I KNOW THERE IS LOVE

GEE VAUCHER

DO YOU THINK I WAS BORN ON THIS WRETCHED EARTH
    for you to govern and kill
        in your stinking factories and offices
            with your stupid systems and skills?
Do you think I've got nothing better to do
    than to grovel in the shit and the crap,
        asking for the bread and home that's mine
            and waiting for a pat on the back?
You think I've got nothing better to do
    than to live in the lie that you give,
        learn the sweet morals, the lessons, the games
            and praise God for the fact that I live?

1982

You took me and made me a MAN by making me strong,
    the power of this land.
You took a woman and taught her she's less,
    a slave to the strong and no more than a guest.
You taught me to love, find a mate and to take
    a woman to serve, but your love is just rape.
You leave me my children to hold and distort,
    to blind with your rules of normality 'til caught.
I give them the food that you sell in the shops,
    I'm told it has goodness when it's only the slops.
You've taken my health with your shitty benevolence,
    you've taken my dignity with your dole queue dependence.
You've taught me to steal when I wanted to share,
    to take for myself and not even care.

You've shifted my vision with oppressive authority,
    the dreams and the hopes nearly fade to strangle me.

You gave me confusion until I had learnt
    to obey all the orders and never get burnt.
I shout in the streets and you take my voice,
    this sham of democracy leaves no choice.
You've taken my eyes 'til there's nothing to see
    except abuse and destruction, no chance to be free.
You've taken my thinking, my means of survival,
    thrust in my hand your gun and your Bible.
You told me to kill for the Lord up above,
    you've given me hate when I KNOW THERE IS LOVE.

1982

WALLS
(FUN IN THE OVEN)
JOY DE VIVRE

DESIRE, DESIRE, DESIRE, DESIRE,
describe, desire, defile, deny.

Defile desire, deny desire,
Describe, describe, describe, describe.

No air to breathe inside your walls,
left to dream inside your walls.

Left us in a wilderness,
well I can make my paradise.

Without your walls I am alive,
no body I in rank and file.

Girl and boy and man and wife,
flesh you measure with a smile.

Have and hold and hold and have,
have and hold and hold and have.

Desire, deny, deny, desire,
have a child to justify.

Images that you apply,
I won't bow my head in shame.

I won't play the game the same,
without your walls I am alive.

Without your walls we all survive,
without your walls no guilt to bear.

Without your love, our love to share,
without your walls I am alive.

Without your walls I am alive.

1979

UPRIGHT CITIZEN

PETE WRIGHT

YOU HAVE THIS LIFE, WHAT FOR? TELL ME.
Spend it on shit, your ignorance appals me.
You serve me your morals, changed for a fiver,
upright citizen, *Penthouse* subscriber.
You won't print the word, but you'll beat up the wife,
in your ignorant, arrogant, terminal life.
You have this life, you deprive me of mine,
with your twisted, imbalanced idea of sin
that revolves around money, how much are you bought for —
a tenner, a fiver, is that what you're caught for?
I'm sick of your pride, you think you can rule me
with crappy judgements from your respectable majority.
Majority of what? You self-oppressed idiot,
I'm not going to carry you, I'm no compatriot.
How many times do I excuse and forgive
the damage inflicted by the way that you live?

I hold my vision against your aggression,
your final defence, your only possession.
I'll show you the blood, but you still point the gun
if the money's enough, or can you show you're a man
to your submissive wife, desperate whore,
home loving, mothering, stifling bore?
You have this life, you twist and abuse it,
morals and money and media controls it.
Can't you see the dead children, blood in the street?
Every fist that you raise is a corpse at your feet.

Every time you are bought, I don't care the amount,
you are the rapist, dealing in death count.
And you do this with mercenary morals, you shit,
oh, you've been told about dignity down in the pit.
Respectable working man, honourable wife?
a waste of energy and an insult to life.

BUY NOW, PAY AS YOU GO

ANNIE ANXIETY

BUY NOW, PAY AS YOU GO,
buy now, say hello.
You can put a mortgage on your life
to enter Shoppers' Paradise.
A trade-in for your dignity.
A lovely colour console TV
to watch and cherish as the days slip by,
and dream of the things that money can buy.

Brushed chrome shit, plastic crap,
my life and my vision is worth more than that.
Plate-glass ghetto, shopping spree;
I'm no fucking commodity.
Lusting for objects, white-wall refrigerator.
Cut off your fingers and buy a vibrator.
Get them while it lasts, your time is running out.
A new mink for Christmas, that's what life's about.

A new tank, a new bomb, awaits you in the store.
Is life all that shallow that you're reaching out for more?
Start planning now for a family plot.
A satin-lined bunker where your corpses can rot.
Well there's nothing for sale here, no day-glo gore,
and I ain't no waxed-up showroom floor whore.
I don't need carrots dangled in front of my eyes,
man-made pre-fab, polyester lies
or sexy glossy adverts left on my mat.

1982

[213]

I live with my needs. I don't need that.
Don't need a yacht to take a cruise.
Don't need a telephone in the loo.
Won't barter my soul for a rip-joint sale.
Excess is just another nouveau jail.
Don't want to grow fat off the fat of the land,
or to choke on the greed of public command.

Work thirty years with one foot in the grave.
Possession junkie, consumer slave.
If money buys freedom, it's already spent.
Your object's the subject of my contempt.
Buy now, pay as you go,
buy now, say hello.
Bye bye.
Buy buy.

1982

SMOTHER LOVE

GEE VAUCHER

THE TRUE ROMANCE IS THE IDEAL REPRESSION,
that you seek, that you dream of, that you look for in the streets,
that you find in the magazines, the cinema, the glossy shops,
and the music spins you round and round looking for the props.

The silken robe, the perfect little ring,
that gives you the illusion when it doesn't mean a thing.
Step outside into the street and staring from the wall
is perfection of the happiness that makes you feel so small.

Romance, can you dance? Do you fit the right description?
Do you love me? Do you love me?
Do you want me for your own?
Say you love me, say you love me,
say you know that I'm the one,
tell me I'm your everything, let us build a home.
We can build a house for us, with little ones to follow,
proof of our normality that justifies tomorrow.

Romance, romance.
Do you love me? Say you do.
We can leave the world behind and make it just for two.
Love don't make the world go round, it holds it right in place,
keeps us thinking love's too pure to see another face.
Love's another skin-trap, another social weapon,
another way to make men slaves and women at their beckon.

1981

Love's another sterile gift, another shit condition
that keeps us seeing just the one and others not existing.
Woman is a holy myth, a gift of man's expression,
she's sweet, defenceless, golden-eyed, a gift of God's repression.

If we didn't have these codes for love, of tokens and positions,
we'd find ourselves as lovers still, not tokens of possessions.
It's a natural, it's a romance, without the power and greed
we can fight to lift the cover if you want to sow a seed.

Do you love me? Do you? Do you?
Don't you see they aim to smother
the actual possibilities of loving all the others?

1981

WHO CAN BE WHO?

PENNY RIMBAUD

DON'T WANT A LIFE OF LIES AND PRETENCE,
don't want to play at attack and defence,
just want my own life, I want to be free
so you can be you, and I can be me.

Respectable businessmen, smart and secure,
eat the fat of the land that they robbed from the poor.
The butcher is smiling as he brings down the knife,
as he cuts up the meat, he thinks of the wife.
As eminent psychiatrists suffer paranoid fits,
the ones they call mad have to pick up the bits.
The preacher speaks calmly, says it's love that we lack
while his imaginary dagger is held at our back.

Don't want a life of lies and pretence,
don't want to play at attack and defence,
just want my own life, I want to be free
so you can be you, and I can be me.

In bed you're the master or mistress, who cares?,
abusing each other as you work off your fears.
Go climb a mountain, go fuck a scout,
avoidance of self is what it's about.
Pretence and illusion to avoid who you are;
don't work on yourself, just polish the car.
Switch on the telly afraid you might find
that as well as a body you've also a mind.

1982

Cheap glossy surface to cover the lie,
cheap easy answers to the what, where, and why.
Media drivel, yet you still watch the screen.
Life ain't for real, it's a magazine.
Conned from the start, but hang onto the lies,
you're a slave to the cathode-ray paradise.
You don't want the world, you just want the pics.
Media junkies, you'd die for a fix.

Don't want a life of lies and pretence,
don't want to play at attack and defence,
just want my own life, I want to be free
so you can be you, and I can be me.

So you say you'll reject it, well that's maybe a start,
but it's so fucking easy to act out a part.
You say you'll reject it, but still toe the line,
conning yourself that you're doing just fine.
Anarchy, freedom, more games to play?
Fight war, not wars? Well it's something to say.
Slogans and badges worn without thought,
instant identities so cheaply bought.
Well freedom ain't product, it isn't just fun,
if you're looking for peace your work's just begun,
fighting oppression, aggression and hate,
fighting warmongers before it's too late.
We've got to fight back to show that we care,
for so many years we've been silenced by fear.
Our lives have been ruined by liars and fools,
the powerful and greedy who bind us with rules,
politicians and preachers who bind us with laws,
who have stolen our peace and given us wars.

They've used us as means to their own violent ends,
turned us against each other, made foes out of friends.
They've distorted, perverted, polluted our lives,
brainwashed the world with their sordid beliefs.
They seek to possess, control and corrupt;
if it's freedom we're after, they've got to be stopped.

1982

BUMHOOLER

PETE WRIGHT

IF THEY DROP A BOMB ON US, WE FUCKING DESERVE IT.
We know we got it coming, we fucking deserve it.
They got a comfy set up, they'll try to preserve it.
We had the early warning, we can sit and observe it.

Sliding down guidelines, cradle to the grave,
all the willing saviours see that we behave.
everybody knows they're there, see them all around,
lots of little people who'll put you in the ground.
Well, take a burning issue and stuff it up your arse.
They've fucked you with a furrowed brow, shitting broken class,
marching down the 'dilly to demonstrate again,
while the men who plan the holocaust
        are pissed out of their brain.
Brain of pasty people who'll bomb it all to fuck,
you can be a victim or they'll let you try your luck.
Pass it on to others, ship it down the line,
leave the world in ruins, you know we've got the time.

If they drop a bomb on us, we fucking deserve it.
We know we got it coming, we fucking deserve it.
They got a comfy set up, they'll try to preserve it.
We had the early warning, we can sit and observe it.

Cop-outs look for motives ... Freudian analyst.
Come on, Mr Horror, what do you make of this?

1982

Won't find many people without their rationale,
any handy concept to hang upon the wall.
Soldier got his enemy,
police have got the State,
family have got home sweet home,
SS got red tape.
MP's got his duty,
priest has got his sin,
everybody finds a hole
to drop somebody in.
Seeking out wisdom in the ironies of life,
weighing up subtleties, fiddling with the ties,
no-one else decides for you whether to or not
you make an easy target if you're running on the spot.

If they drop a bomb on us, we fucking deserve it.
We know we got it coming, we fucking deserve it.
They got a comfy set up, they'll try to preserve it.
We had the early warning, we can sit and observe it.

Someone's been training, flexing their muscles,
getting in practice, irrelevant tussles.
Given a march, or a quiet Sunday demo,
they wait till the State puts the finger on you.

Peeping through a frown, your humanity in rags,
playing the loser 'til the sense of purpose sags.
They can deal with heroes, watch the bleeders run,
it's only your head keeps the target from the gun.
No-one else decides for you, whether to or not,
You make an easy target, if you're running on the spot...

1982

YOU'RE ALREADY DEAD

PENNY RIMBAUD

PACIFIED. CLASSIFIED. KEEP IN LINE. YOU'RE DOING FINE.
Lost your voice? There ain't no choice.
Play the game silent and tame.
Be the passive observer, sit back and look
    at the world they destroyed and the peace they took.
Ask no questions, hear no lies
    and you'll be living in the comfort of a fool's paradise.
         You're already dead.

If you're the passive observer, here's a message for you ...
         you're already dead.
Afraid to do what you know you should do ...
         you're already dead.
The world's at the edge of nuclear destruction,
but you're too afraid to make the connection.
You still believe the system's there for your protection ...
         you're already dead.

By letting it happen without a fight ...
         you're already dead.
With your endless debates about wrong and right ...
         you're already dead.
Nothing's going to change if you're not prepared to act,
there's no point complaining after the fact,
content to be a number,
branded X and neatly packed ...
         you're already dead.

1984

Four hundred thousand people marched for CND...
                    they're already dead.
unless they're willing to act on what they see...
                    they're already dead.
If each and every one of us was prepared to fight for more,
to stand against the system that creates the need for war,
the élite would have to run like it's never run before...
                    they're already dead.

We don't need organising or politicians being patronising.
We don't need leadership,
trendy lefties being hip.
Don't need their condescension
        or their back to the roots pretension.
We've heard it all before,
politicians saying 'no more war',
pulling wool across our eyes.
We don't need their dangerous lies.
We won't accept capitulation,
it's just manipulation.
They want the smooth without the rough,
but words and gestures aren't enough.
We've got to learn to reject all leaders
        and the passive shit they feed us...
                    they're already dead.

If you think moderation's going to pave the way to peace...
                    you're already dead.
What good is moderation 'gainst the army and police?
                    you're already dead.
We're not promoting mindless violence,
keep that for the fools,

1984

we're simply saying be prepared to break their laws and rules,
let them know the bigger they come,
the harder they will fall ...

                they're already dead.

If they're going to play it dirty,
so are we ...

                they're already dead.
They can keep their lies about the land of the free ...

                they're already dead.
We've allowed them too often to use their iron fist,
but there's one little detail they appear to have missed ...
you don't have to be PASSIVE just because you're a PACIFIST ...

                they're already dead.

They'll try to sell their system
    like it's some kind of age-old wisdom,
but we've been had like that before,
it's the rich exploiting the poor.
Well here's an honest confession,
we think it's time they learnt a lesson.
They've tried to hold the people down,
but we've simply gone underground,
moving in the darkness looking for the light,
looking for the future and ready to fight,
looking for the freedom that's been denied,
fast to attack and fast to hide.
In a world where the people can't make it,
they've simply got to learn to break it
    and if the wealthy aren't prepared to shake it ...
OK, we'll simply have to take it ...

                you're already dead.

1984

BLOODY REVOLUTIONS

PENNY RIMBAUD

YOU TALK ABOUT YOUR REVOLUTION, WELL, THAT'S FINE,
but what are you going to be doing come the time?
Are you going to be the big man with the tommy gun?
Will you talk of freedom when the blood begins to run?
Well, freedom has no value if violence is the price;
don't want your revolution, I want anarchy and peace.

You talk of overthrowing power with violence as your tool,
you speak of liberation and when the people rule,
well ain't it people rule right now, what difference would there be?
Just another set of bigots with their rifle-sights on me.

1980

But what about those people who don't want your new restrictions,
those who disagree with you and have their own convictions?
You say they've got it wrong because they don't agree with you,
so when the revolution comes you'll have to run them through,
yet you say that revolution will bring freedom for us all,
well freedom just ain't freedom when your back's against the wall.

You talk of overthrowing power with violence as your tool,
you speak of liberation and when the people rule,
well ain't it people rule right now, what difference would there be?
Just another set of bigots with their rifle-sights on me.

Will you indoctrinate the masses to serve your new regime
and simply do away with those whose views are too extreme?
Transportation details could be left to British Rail;
where Zyklon B succeeded, North Sea Gas will fail.

It's just the same old story of man destroying man,
we've got to look for other answers to the problems of this land.

You talk of overthrowing power with violence as your tool,
you speak of liberation and when the people rule,
well ain't it people rule right now, what difference would there be?
Just another set of bigots with their rifle-sights on me.

> *Vive la revolution, people of the world unite,*
> *stand up men of courage, it's your job to fight.*

It all seems very easy, this revolution game,
but when you start to really play, things won't be quite the same.
Your intellectual theories on how it's going to be
don't seem to take into account the true reality,
'cos the truth of what you're saying as you sit there sipping beer,
is pain and death and suffering, but of course you wouldn't care.
You're far too much of a man for that, if Mao did it so can you.
What's the freedom of us all against the suffering of the few?
That's the kind of self-deception that killed ten million Jews,
just the same false logic that all power-mongers use.

So don't think you can fool me with your political tricks,
political right, political left, you can keep your politics,
government is government, and all government is force,
left or right, right or left, it takes the same old course.
Oppression and restriction, regulation, rule and law,
the seizure of that power is all your revolution's for.
You romanticise your heroes, quote from Marx and Mao,
well their ideas of freedom are just oppression now.

1980

Nothing's changed for all the death that their ideas created,
it's just the same fascistic games, but the rules aren't clearly stated.
Nothing's really different, 'cos all government's the same,
they can call it freedom, but slavery is the game.

There's nothing that you offer, but a dream of last years hero,
the truth of revolution, brother,
                          brother,
                                brother,
                                     brother,
                                          is year zero.

1980

GENERAL BACARDI

PENNY RIMBAUD

I'VE SEEN IT ALL BEFORE, REVOLUTION AT MY BACK DOOR,
    well who's to say it won't happen all again?
The generals sip Bacardi,
    while the privates feel the pain.

They talk from the screen and TV tube,
    they talk revolution like it's processed food.
They talk anarchy from music hall stages,
    look for change in colour supplement pages.

They think that by talking from some distant tower
    that something might change in the structure of power.
They dream, they dream,
    never stand on their feet.

Alternative values were a con, a fucking con.
They never really meant it when they said, *Get it on*.
They really meant, *Mine, that's mine*, can't you see?
They stamped on our heads so that they could be free.

They formed little groups, like rich man's ghettos,
    tending their goats and organic tomatoes.
While the world was being fucked by fascist regimes,
    they talked of windmills and psychedelic dreams.

1978

DRY WEATHER

EVE LIBERTINE AND PENNY RIMBAUD

IS THERE ANYONE PREPARED TO TELL ME WHY,
  tell me why I'm being sucked dry?
Oh yes, that is yours and this is mine,
  as long as the balance is out, that's fine.
I don't define the terms of the oppression,
  do you awake to that dull and grey depression?
You ride on me,
  suck my energy.

You take what you want when you want it,
  you reject any change that I make.
You ask me for more when I've spent it,
  when I've given it all, you still take.
Oh yes I know the lines you draw are for protection,
  the number given for a name is simply for detection.
I know I'm only paper in a file,
  but couldn't you treat me as a human for a while?
You offer your protection, but insist when I decline,
  you offer independence, but demand I toe the line.
You say you give me freedom, but you hang on to the key,
  well don't you think, perhaps, the decision's up to me?
So tell me I'm dreaming if I want to live,
  and I'll tell you you're just scheming to make me give
    more than I want to, more than I can;
    you don't want person, you just want woman.
You hide behind logic, secure with your facts,
  you've a history of time to back up your claims,
    protecting the future by filling up the cracks,
    that might expose the real nature of your games.

[229]

1981

You want woman 'cos she's children for your system,
        well, people wither in that living death.
You hide behind your prejudice, afraid of my wisdom,
        afraid I might question your unquestioned worth.
Is there anyone prepared to tell me why,
        tell me why I'm being sucked dry?

                Used as a tool?
                        Treated as a fool?

        Spat on?
                Shat on?
Totally confused?

                Fucked up?
                        Mucked up?
        Totally abused?

                Pulled about?
                        Fooled about?
        Treated like a toy?

        Joked about?
                Poked about?
Something to destroy?

        Tricked?
                Kicked?
        I don't want these games.

SHAVED WOMEN

ANNIE ANXIETY

SCREAMING BABIES,
screaming babies,
screaming babies,
screaming babies.

Shaved women collaborators,
shaved women are they traitors?
Dead bodies all around.

Screaming babies,
screaming babies,
screaming babies,
screaming babies.

Shaved women instigators,
shaved women shooting dope,
shaved women disco dancing.

Screaming babies,
screaming babies,
screaming babies,
screaming babies.

In all your decadence people die.
In all your decadence people die.
In all our decadence people die.
In all your decadence people die.

G'S SONG

GEE VAUCHER

THIS COUNTRY TELLS US THAT WE'RE DOWN AND OUT,
got you thinking that we're through.
Got to suffer to get them moving,
say it's up to me and you.

But look around and you'll see who gets the goods,
not you and me,
'cos they ain't suffering,
no, not for us.
They're masquerading like pissers must.

They abuse us,
keep us right underfoot
with the illusion of contentment and good,
but it's not over,
war's still around.
They've got no problem when you're underground.

1978

YOU PAY

YOU'RE PAYING FOR PRISONS,
you're paying for war,
you're paying for lobotomies,
you're paying for law,
you're paying for their order,
you're paying for their murder,
you're paying for your ticket to watch the farce.

Knowing you've made your contribution
to the systems fucked solution,
to their political pollution,
no chance of revolution,
no chance of change,
you've got no range.

Don't just take it,
don't take their shit,
don't play their game,
don't take their blame,
USE YOUR OWN HEAD,
your turn instead.

It's not economise,
it's not apologise,
it's not make do,
it's not pull through,
it's not take it,

1978

it's not make it,
it's not just you,
it's not just madmen,
it's not difficult,
it's not behave,
it's not, *oh well, just this once*,
it's fucking impossible,
it's fucking unbearable,
it's fucking stupid,
IT'S FUCKING STUPID.

SECURICOR

PETE WRIGHT

I'M A PRIVATE IN A PRIVATE ARMY,
I'm a private in a private army,
I'm a private in a private army,
I'm a private in a private army.

I am a-working for Securicor,
 take the money and come back for more.
I want to do it 'cos I know I should,
 for the customer and the common good.

I walk around with a big alsatian,
 he'll re-arrange you with no provocation.
And I'm the bugger who has got the lead,
 you'll have to be right if you want to get at me.

Securicor cares,
Securicor cares,
Securicor scares the shit out of you.
Do you want to come closer?

I block the pavement with my club and hat,
 I deal in money that you can't get at.
You want to use me 'cos I'm up for rent,
 tough shit, 'cos I'm really busy.

1978

You ought to know me 'cos I've been a cop,
   out of the army where I learned the lot.
Some kids still chuckle when they see my van,
   but it's not all money, sonny, you want to come closer?

Securicor cares,
Securicor cares,
Securicor scares the shit out of you.
Do you want to come closer? Do you want to come closer?

I'm a private in a private army,
I'm a private in a private army,
I'm a private in a private army,
I'm a private in a private army.

1978

WHAT A SHAME

PETE WRIGHT

IT DOESN'T TAKE MUCH TO BRING YOU DOWN,
there are plenty of people standing round,
they wait till you slacken off just a bit,
then they fill you up with passive bullshit.

It's too good.
It can't last.
What a shame.

Watch out for the quiet ones at the back,
all they want is the smallest crack.
Everything's happening down the front,
innocent bystander, you're the biggest runt.

Fuck the punks.
Punks are fucked.
It's too loud.
Awful row.
They can't play.
They'll give up
in the end.
What a shame.

Oh what a shame, it's still the same.
That's what you think.

Watch out for the quiet ones at the back,
all they want is the smallest crack.
Everything's happening down the front.
Innocent bystander you're the biggest runt.

We all know
it's so bad,
but we say so.
WHAT A SHAME.

1978

RIVAL TRIBAL REBEL REVEL (PT.2)

PENNY RIMBAUD

COR BLIMEY GUVNOR I'M THE BIG 'UN,
cop an eyeful of this muscular arm.
Being tough 'n' rough is my kind of fun, but, of course,
I never do no harm.
It ain't my fault I like cracking bones,
it gives me a funny kind of thrill,
and I can't help smiling at the pathetic moans
as I go in for the kill.

Tribal wars are raging, it's a battlefield in the street,
there's games to play and hell to pay,
when the rival tribal rebels meet.

Why can't people just leave me be?
I can't help doing what I do,
but I'll DO anybody who ain't like me, so forget your what,
why or who.
I ain't got no purpose and I don't give a fuck,
I never asked for this life.
If you're looking for reasons you're out of luck,
I'll just show you the point with my knife.

Tribal wars are raging, no-one's safe out on their own,
the gangs are about and they scream and shout,
so you'd better not be caught alone.

I did it 'cos there ain't nothing else to do,
there ain't nowhere'll let me in.
It ain't my fault I want to hurt and screw,
so I've destroyed every place where I've been.
I had trouble at the local so they won't serve me there,
I just had to chivvy up this bloke,
I left him with a smile cut from ear to ear,
but the bleeder never got the joke.
I used to have a bird, but I put her up the spout,
so I had to tell her where to get off.
Well, you can't blame me if I want to get about,
if you're a man you've got to be tough.
I used to go down the café for tea,
but my boot got attacked by the door,
so now it ain't open for the likes of me
and we're back on the streets like before.

Tribal wars are raging, our heroes are standing tall,
but the truth of the matter
if you cut out the patter,
is that pride always comes before the fall.

They can stand on the corner with their violence and their hate,
stand there and fester 'til they've left it too late
to realise it's themselves they've put there on the spot
'cos they've wasted the one and only life that they've got.

Tribal wars are raging, everyone's just acting out bad parts.
Hey there, big man,
take a look at yourself,
it's in the mirror that the real war starts.

WHO'S SIDE YOU ON?

STEVE IGNORANT

READ THE EVENING PAPERS
    about the National Front,
they go out and they do it,
    they're such a bunch of cunts.
They make safety-pins,
    of silver and gold,
the bastards who buy them,
    they know what they've been sold.

    Who's side you on?   Who's side you on?
    Who's side you on?   Major General Despair,
                       Major General Despair.

1978

The ex-Wing Commander
    who's confronting you
with school, church and your mama;
    play his game and you're fucked.
Now be reasonable,
    respecting the law,
    so where does it get you, you've been there before,
                      remember?
    Who's side you on?   Who's side you on?
    Who's side you on?   Major General Despair,
                       Major General Despair.

    Who's side you on?
    Who's side you on?
    Who's side you on?
    Who's side you on?   Get in line.
    Who's side you on?   Get in line.

[241]

MEDIA BAG

PETE WRIGHT

WE BURN OUR MISTAKES AND WE WATCH AS THEY BURN,
we've been here so long we've got nothing to learn,
and we put all the nastiest bits in your media bag.

Angela Rippon,
Kenneth Kendal,
Robert Dougal,
Richard Baker;
we put all the nastiest shits in your media bag.

Feel pretty solid, can move pretty smooth,
yeah, but I'm learning I've got nothing to lose,
and you put all the nastiest licks in your media slag.

Fucking watch out.
I am about.
I can and I don't have to pretend anymore.

1978

I AIN'T THICK, IT'S JUST A TRICK

PENNY RIMBAUD

OH YEAH? OH YEAH?
Well I've got it all up here, see?
Oh yeah? Oh yeah?
When they think they've got it all out there, see?
They can fuck off,
they ain't got me,
they can't buy my dignity.
Oh yeah, oh yeah,
let me tell you
I've got it up here, see?

They tried to get me with a TV show,
but I wouldn't have none of it, no, no, no.
Standards and values on a black and white screen,
Sarah Farah Fawcett acting mean.
She's got the lot, that's what they want you to think,
but read between the lines, you'll see the missing link.
She's just a fucking puppet in their indoctrination plan,
"be like me girls, become a real man,"
live to the full, always act flash,
don't use your brains when the body makes the splash.

They tried to get me in the supermarket store,
bought what I wanted, then they said "buy more."
Mountains of crap that nobody really needs,
gaily coloured wrappers to suit assorted greeds.

They've got the lot, that's what they want you to think,
read between the lines, you'll see the missing link.
Buy this product, pay for the crap,
a quarter for the product, three quarters for the wrap.
Be a happy family like the people on the pack,
pay up to the profit-makers, you'll never look back.

They tried to get me with their learning and their books,
deep understanding and intelligent looks,
but all of the time, they never saw me,
they were just looking for what they wanted to see.
They've got the lot, that's what they want you to think,
read between the lines, you'll see the missing link.
The books are easy back-ups for what they want to do to you,
bind you up in slavery for the privileged few,
they'll prove their lies with history, say "that's the way it always was,
accept the shit and serfdom, be one of us."

They tried to get me with religion and with Christ,
said I'd get to heaven if I acted real nice,
but they were just preparing a crucifix for me,
a life of guilt, of sin, of pain, of holy misery.
They've got the lot, that's what they want you to think,
read between the lines, you'll see the missing link.
The Bible's just a blueprint of their morality scene,
just another load of shit on how it's never been.
They stand there in the pulpit, doling out their lies,
offering forgiveness, then they talk of eyes for eyes.

1979

They try to get me, but I won't be got,
they say I'm a misfit, I say I'm not,
I never set out to profit from another,
those smarmy bastards would steal from their mother.
They've got the lot, that's what they want you to think,
read between the lines, you'll see the missing link.
They plundered and slaughtered in the name of truth,
acceptance of normality is what they want from you as proof.
They think they've got the answers,
but there's one thing that they miss,
their cup which overfloweth is just full of piss.

1979

BANNED FROM THE ROXY

PENNY RIMBAUD

BANNED FROM THE ROXY ... OKAY,
I never liked playing there anyway.
They said they only wanted well behaved boys;
do they think guitars and microphones
are just fucking toys?
Fuck 'em, I've chosen to make my stand
against what I feel is wrong with this land;
they just sit there on their over-fed arses
feeding off the sweat of less fortunate classes.
They keep their fucking power 'cos their finger's on the button,
they've got control and won't let it be forgotten.
The truth of their reality's the wrong end of a gun,
the proof of that is Belfast and that's no fucking fun.
Seeing the squaddy lying in the front yard,
seeing the machine guns resting on the fence,
finding the entrance to your own front door is barred,
and they've got the fucking nerve to call that defence.
Seems that their defence is just the threat of strength,
protection for the privileged at any length,
the government defending their profits from the poor,
the rich and the fortunate chaining up the door,
afraid that the people may ask for just a little more
than the shit they get,
    the shit they get,
    the shit they get,
    the shit they get,

1978

the shit they get,
the shit they get,
the shit they get,
the shit they get.
DEFENCE? SHIT. IT'S NOTHING LESS THAN WAR,
AND NO ONE BUT THE GOVERNMENT KNOWS
WHAT THE FUCK IT'S FOR.

Oh yes, they say it's defence, say it's decency,
My Lai, Hiroshima, know what I mean?
The same fucking lies with depressing frequency.
They say "We had to do it to keep our lives clean".
Well whose life? Whose fucking life?
Who the fuck are they talking to?
Whose life? Whose fucking life?
I tell you one thing, it ain't me and you.

And their systems? Christ, they're everywhere;
school, army, church, the corporation deal,
a fucked-up reality, based on fear,
a fucking conspiracy to stop you feeling real.
Well they're wrong, ain't got me.
I'll say they're fucking wrong.
I ain't quite ready with my gun,
but I got my fucking song ...
banned from the Roxy ... well, okay,
I never much liked playing there anyway ...
GUNS!

1978

DO THEY OWE US A LIVING?

STEVE IGNORANT

FUCK THE POLITICALLY MINDED,
here's something I want to say
about the state of the nation,
the way it treats us today.
At school they give you shit,
drop you in the pit,
you try and try and try to get out,
but you can't
because they've fucked you about.
Then you're a prime example
of how they must not be.
This is just a sample
of what they've done
to you and me.

Do they owe us a living?   Of course they do, of course they do.
Do they owe us a living?   Of course they do, of course they do.
Do they owe us a living?   OF COURSE THEY FUCKING DO.

They don't want me anymore
'cos I threw it on the floor.
They used to call me sweet thing,
but I'm nobody's plaything,
and now that I am different
they'd love to bust my head,
love to see me cop-out,
they'd love to see me dead.

1978

Do they owe us a living?   Of course they do, of course they do.
Do they owe us a living?   Of course they do, of course they do.
Do they owe us a living?   OF COURSE THEY FUCKING DO.

The living that is owed to me
I'm never going to get.
They've buggered this old world up,
up to their necks in debt.
They'd give you a lobotomy
for something you ain't done.
They'll make you an epitome
of everything that's wrong.

Do they owe us a living?   Of course they do, of course they do.
Do they owe us a living?   Of course they do, of course they do.
Do they owe us a living?   OF COURSE THEY FUCKING DO.

1978

Don't take any notice
of what the public think,
they're so hyped up with TV
they just don't want to think.
They'll use you as a target
for demands and for advice.
When you don't want to hear it
they'll say you're full of vice.

Do they owe us a living?   Of course they do, of course they do.
Do they owe us a living?   Of course they do, of course they do.
Do they owe us a living?   OF COURSE THEY FUCKING DO.

ASYLUM

PENNY RIMBAUD

I AM NO FEEBLE CHRIST, NOT ME.
He hangs in glib delight upon his cross,
    above my body.
Christ, forgive.
    FORGIVE?
I vomit for you, Jesu.
Shit forgive.
Down now from your cross.
Down now from your papal heights,
    from that churlish suicide, petulant child.
Down from those pious heights,
    royal flag-bearer, goat, billy.
I vomit for you.
Forgive?
Shit he forgives.
He hangs in crucified delight, nailed to the extent of his vision,
    his cross,
    his manhood,
    violence,
        guilt,
            sin.
He would nail my body upon his cross,
    suicide visionary,
    death reveller,
    rake,
        rapist,
            lifefucker,

1978

Jesu,

earthmover,

Christus,

gravedigger.

You dug the graves of Auschwitz,
the soil of Treblinka is your guilt,

your sin.

Master,

master of gore,

enigma.

You carry the standard of our oppression.
Enola is your gaiety.
The bodies of Hiroshima are your delight.
The nails are the only trinity,

hold them in your corpsey gracelessness,

the image I have had to suffer.
The cross is the virgin body of womanhood that you defile.
You nail yourself to your own sin.
Lame-arse Jesus calls me brother;

there are no words for my contempt.
Every woman is a cross in his filthy theology,

his arrogant delight.
He turns his back upon me in his fear.
He dare not face me.
Fearfucker.
Share nothing, you Christ:

sterile,

impotent,

fucklove prophet of death.
You are the ultimate pornography,

in your cuntfear,

cockfear,

                    manfear,
                womanfear,
                    unfair,
                            warfare,
                            warfare,
                            warfare,
                            warfare,
                            warfare,
                            warfare,
                            warfare,
                            warfare.

JESUS DIED FOR HIS OWN SINS,
NOT MINE.

1978

THE SOUND OF FREE SPEECH

PENNY RIMBAUD

1978

1978

10 NOTES ON A SUMMER'S DAY
— THE SWAN SONG —

PENNY RIMBAUD

I

Touch me with normality,
a childhood I never had.
      I too might have stood Aryan
      in the seeding grasses,
      applauded by the bigots
      who sneer at the sight of me.
Age is no comfort,
indeed the options narrow.
      The prison door is closed,
      locked by their prejudice
      and my simple desire
      to live in a different way.
We cannot conform,
indeed the options narrow.

1984

In the Academy we sat,
learned like fools.
We read predictability as if it were wisdom.
>   My head bows.
>   I see sunlight glint
>   across the wooden panels.
>   "If only we were free."
Such a timid whisper against the scratch of pen.
Two thousand years these histories have been documented:
equation and formula,
static laws.
>   I turn from my books, volumes lay empty
>   and so too is the Academy.
>   Whatever life there might have been within
>   has slipped away, into the sunlight.

1984

3

Petulance is a pretty girl
dabbling on the river's bank.
Alice holds posies,
sensual rosaries.
>   The daisy chain,
>   the daisy chain,
hunger child and lazy brain.
>   Petulance is a pretty girl,
>   dawdling by the river's bank.
She squashes cold matter from the head of a tiny newt.
>   What is that if it is not grey?

4

Darkness is a game we lazily play,
we suck on paradise as we would the peach stone…
all is extracted but the life:
childhood dreams cursed with the filthy garbage
of realisation,
so clean in imagination,
clear as memory,
so clean in imagination.
We hide in the gaps as if their use as shitholes
was unknown to us.

5

Oh how we laughed at awkwardness and inability:
stabs in the back of consciousness.
We saw the pigs stranglehold our comrades
and ran sickened from the scene.
Some remained to share.
Nausea. Nausea.
We were invited to the cocktail party
and suffered loathsome toasts.
We tasted the melancholy
and the awful empty laugh of the socialite.
Nausea.
Get back. Get back.
Get back. Get back.
Tasteful slants of teacup,
finely pointed fingers,
skywards.
Is this a warning?
Nausea.

6

And if on my blood you created this free society,
 what then?
Would your stupid petty prejudice
still push you into maliciousness?
Isn't the earth already at peace?
Are not we, as separate personalities,
the only warring faction?
I suggest togetherness,
proclaiming my love and compassion,
will you make that into commodity,
asset and possession?

7

We trained in the art of tragedy,
taking sidelines, consumed by its ethic.
            Consumed, oh consumed.
We announced amnesty,
saw ourselves as reflections.
            Oh my military boy,
                swathed in darkness and death.
We search out each other's name
in the horrid graveyard.
            Consumed, oh consumed.

1984

8

If you stop and ask "What now? Where now?"
    do you really expect an answer?
Is it not simply your own conscience
from which you seek a reply?
I can only say this or that,
and hope that we might strike a common chord.
      Meanwhile we learn more of ourselves
      and parts of each other.

9

We ate vanity pancakes,
amused by our self-image.
      Who'd have thought it possible
      that the chimps could brew their own tea?

1984

10

Those dark shadows move as if guided by some hand.
Where the sea beats mercilessly on the shore,
there is the security of the land.
At the sea's deepest point there is often a strange calm.

CRASS *were*:

STEVE IGNORANT · VOCALS

EVE LIBERTINE · VOCALS

JOY DE VIVRE · VOCALS

PHIL FREE · LEAD GUITAR

B A NANA · RHYTHM GUITAR

PETE WRIGHT · BASS

PENNY RIMBAUD · DRUMS

GEE VAUCHER · VISUALS

joined intermittently by:

MICK DUFFIELD · FILM-MAKER

ANNIE ANXIETY · POET

INDEX

10 Notes On A Summer's Day 255
Acts Of Love 1
Angels 200
Asylum 250
Banned From The Roxy 246
Bata Motel 145
Beg Your Pardon 120
Berkertex Bribe 139
Big A Little A 57
Big Man, Big M.A.N. 172
Birth Control 'n' Rock 'n' Roll 125
Bloody Revolutions 225
Bumhooler 220
Buy Now Pay As You Go 213
Chairman Of The Bored 205
Contaminational Power 166
Crutch Of Society 182
Darling 131
Deadhead 185
Demoncrats 164
Do They Owe Us A Living? 248
Don't Get Caught 148
Don't Tell Me You Care 98
Dry Weather 229
End Result 203
Fight War Not Wars 163
Fun Going On 197
G's Song 232
Gasman Cometh, The 183
General Bacardi 228
Gotcha! 106
Greatest Working Class Rip-Off, The 188
Have A Nice Day 113
Health Surface 174
Heard Too Much About 187
How Does It Feel? 92
Hurry Up Garry 191
I Ain't Thick, It's Just A Trick 243
I Know There Is Love 207
Immortal Death, The 95
Major General Despair 160
Media Bag 242

Message To Thatcher … , A 60
Mother Earth 132
Mother Love 134
Nagasaki Is Yesterday's Dogend 111
Nagasaki Nightmare 129
Nineteen Eighty Bore 115
Our Wedding 138
Poison In A Pretty Pill 136
Punk Is Dead 127
Reality Asylum 51
Reality Whitewash 123
Reject Of Society 201
Rival Tribal Rebel Revel 180
Rival Tribal Rebel Revel (Pt.2) 239
Securicor 235
Sentiment (White Feathers) 158
Shaved Women 231
Sheep Farming In The Falklands 102
Smash The Mac 141
Smother Love 215
So What? 168
Sound Of Free Speech, The 253
Sucks 199
System 171
Systematic Death 151
They've Got A Bomb 154
Time Out 195
Tired 178
Upright Citizen 211
Walls 209
What A Shame 237
What The Fuck? 117
Where Next Columbus? 54
White Punks On Hope 193
Who Dunnit? 108
Who's Side You On? 241
Women 119
Yes, Sir, I Will 63
You Can Be Who? 217
You Pay 233
You're Already Dead 222
You've Got Big Hands 176

FURTHER READING

SHIBBOLETH
PENNY RIMBAUD AKA JJ RATTER
AK Press, 1998 · ISBN 1-873176-40-6
Autobiography.

. . .

THE DIAMOND SIGNATURE &
THE DEATH OF IMAGINATION
JJ RATTER AKA PENNY RIMBAUD
AK Press, 1999 · ISBN 1-873176-55-4
The published unpublishable work.

. . .

CRASS ART AND OTHER PRE
POST-MODERNIST MONSTERS
GEE VAUCHER
AK Press, 1999 · ISBN 1-873176-10-4
Art.

. . .

'Where Crass voluntarily blow their own' can be accessed at:
http://www.southern.com/southern/band/crass/index.html
official site run by Southern Records, distributors of Crass Records.
The site contains a great deal of information and archive material.

FURTHER LISTENING

—— *Long Players* ——

THE FEEDING OF THE 5000	621984
STATIONS OF THE CRASS	521984
PENIS ENVY	321984
CHRIST — THE ALBUM	BOLLOX 2U2
YES SIR, I WILL	121984/2
ACTS OF LOVE	1984/4
BEST BEFORE 1984	CAT.NO.5

—— *7"* ——

REALITY ASYLUM	521984
BLOODY REVOLUTIONS	421984/1
NAGASAKI NIGHTMARE	421984/5
RIVAL TRIBAL REBEL REVEL	421984/6
OUR WEDDING	ENVY 1
MERRY CRASSMAS	COLD TURKEY 1
HOW DOES IT FEEL?	221984/6
SHEEP FARMING IN THE FALKLANDS	121984/3
WHO DUNNIT?	121984/4
YOU'RE ALREADY DEAD	1984

—— *12"* ——

10 NOTES ON A SUMMER'S DAY	CAT.NO.6

Vinyl re-issues of Crass albums, presented in the superbly designed packaging by Gee Vaucher, are now available along with CD editions; available from either your local independent record shop or direct from the distributor:

SOUTHERN RECORDS · PO BOX 59 · LONDON · N22 1AR

POMONA BOOKS

POMONA'S AIM IS TO PRODUCE A CLASSIC BRANDING OF TITLES, each of them beautifully presented and immediately identifiable to readers. We will publish the work of stimulating and talented authors. Our website is www.pomonauk.com

Also available:

FOOTNOTE*
by Boff Whalley

ISBN 1-904590-00-4

£8.99

FOOTNOTE IS CLEVER, FUNNY AND IRREVERENT — A STORY ABOUT A boy from the redbrick clichés of smalltown England reconciling Mormonism and punk rock, industrial courtesy and political insurrection.

He finds a guitar, anarchism and art terrorism and, after years (and years and years) of earnest, determined, honest-to-goodness slogging, his pop group† makes it big; that's BIG with a megaphone actually. They write a song that has the whole world singing and, funnily enough, it's an admirable summary of a life well lived — about getting knocked down and getting back up again.

Meanwhile, there's a whole world still happening: authentic lives carefully drawn, emotional but not sentimental and always with a writer's eye for detail. *Footnote* is not another plodding rock memoir but a compassionate, critical and sometimes cynical account of a life steeped in pop culture, lower division football and putting the world to rights.

---

* See page 293 of Boff Whalley's book.

† Boff Whalley is a member of Chumbawamba.

RULE OF NIGHT
by Trevor Hoyle

ISBN 1-904590-01-2

£8.99

IF THE SIXTIES WERE SWINGING, THE SEVENTIES WERE THE HANG-
over — darker, nastier, uglier — especially if you lived on a council estate in
the north of England.

Rule of Night was first published in 1975 and has since become a cult
classic. It pre-dates the current vogue for 'hard men' and 'football hoolie'
books by 25 years.

It is, however, much more than this. Trevor Hoyle creates a chillingly
detailed world, where teenagers prowl rainy fluorescent-lit streets dressed
as their *Clockwork Orange* anti-heroes. The backdrop is provided by Ford
Cortinas, Players No.6, the factory, the relentless struggle to maintain hope.

Hoyle, who has since been published by John Calder (home to Samuel
Beckett and William S. Burroughs), has added a fascinating afterword to
his original book which has been out of print and highly sought-after for
many years.

THE FAN
by Hunter Davies

ISBN 1-904590-02-0

£9.99

HUNTER DAVIES IS ONE OF BRITAIN'S MOST ACCLAIMED WRITERS and journalists. He has written over 30 books, among them modern classics, *The Beatles* and *A Walk Around The Lakes*. *The Glory Game*, published in 1972, is a benchmark work on football and is still in print today.

The Fan is a collection of very personal, unusual pieces about his life as a supporter. He observes football in its sovereignty of the late 1900s and early 2000s and tackles the big topics of the day: Beckham's haircuts, high finance, the price of pies, the size of match day programmes, the enormous wages, the influence of Sky TV, England's numerous managers.

Along the way, he also lets us into his home life, in London and the Lake District, his family, his work, his tortoise, his poorly knee (caused by too much Sunday football).

Originally published in the *New Statesman* magazine, *The Fan* catches Davies at his very best and most amusing. It will appeal to supporters of any age, sex and loyalties.

POMONA SOUNDS

POMONA SOUNDS IS OUR AFFILIATED RECORD LABEL.
The following CD albums will enhance your life:

PS-001	The Rosenbergs *Ameripop*	£7
PS-002	Black September *Black September*	£10
PS-003	Mudskipper *Eggshells*	£10
PS-004	The Monkey Run *Escape From The Rake*	£10
PS-005	Crass *You'll Ruin It For Everyone*	£10
PS-006	Killing Stars *When The Light First Fell*	£10
PS-007	Black September *You Can Do Anything*	
	If You Set Your Mind To It	£10

· · ·

All Pomona books and CDs should be available through your friendly local bookseller or record store. If yours isn't so friendly, and you would like to order direct, please send a cheque, including postage, made payable to 'Pomona' and mail to:

Pomona
P.O. Box 50, Hebden Bridge, West Yorks HX7 8WA, England, UK
www.pomonauk.com

POST & PACKING RATES:
UK £1.50 per item
Europe £2.50 per item
Elsewhere £3.50 per item

YOU'LL RUIN IT FOR EVERYONE

CRASS

POMONA SOUNDS PS-005

£10.00

AUTHORISED LIVE CD, WITH FULL COLOUR SLEEVE AND 16-PAGE booklet. A document of Crass' riotous concert at The Lesser City Hall, Perth, Scotland on 4th July 1981.

Punk Is Dead

Nagasaki Nightmare

Darling

Mother Earth

Reality Whitewash

Heard Too Much About

System

Big Man, Big M.A.N.

Health Surface

Big A Little A

You've Got Big Hands

Tired

Rival Tribal Rebel Revel

Poison In A Pretty Pill

Berkertex Bribe

They've Got A Bomb

Public Service Announcement

[You are listening to Radio Two]

Attention please … attention please … attention
please … attention please …

    Here is a special announcement.
    Attention please …
    here is a special announcement:

It is with very deep regret
that we have to announce to you,
contrary to claims made
by some members of the general public,
that PUNK IS DEAD.